We the People

Indiana

and the

United States Constitution

Lectures in Observance of the
Bicentennial of the Constitution

PATRICK J. FURLONG
ALAN T. NOLAN
KENNETH R. STEVENS
EMMA LOU THORNBROUGH
IRVING L. FINK
DAVID RAY PAPKE

Indianapolis
Indiana Historical Society
1987

Library of Congress Cataloging-in-Publication Data

We the people.

   Lectures given under the sponsorship of the Indiana
Association of Historians.
   Includes bibliographies and index.
   Contents: The South Bend fugitive slave cases / by
Patrick J. Furlong—Ex parte Milligan : a curb of
executive and military power / by Alan T. Nolan—
The Kinsey customs case and constitutional law / by
Kenneth R. Stevens—[etc.]
   1. United States—Constitutional law.   2. Law—
Indiana—History and criticism.   I. Furlong, Patrick
Joseph, 1940–   .   II. Indiana Historical Society.
III. Indiana Association of Historians.
KF4550.A2W37   1987   349.772   86–27175
ISBN 0–87195–007–3 (pbk.) 347.72

Contents

Introduction

This book consists of six lectures given under the sponsorship of the Indiana Association of Historians in observance of the Bicentennial of the United States Constitution. It is hoped that the lectures, dealing as they do with constitutionally significant cases which arose in Indiana, will help to bring some of the great constitutional issues close to home and create an awareness of the Constitution as a vital, living instrument of government. Although historical in content, the lectures raise questions which have significance for our own times. Except for *Ex parte Milligan* the cases are seldom mentioned in books on constitutional history, but, disparate as they are, they are representative of the constitutional development of the United States as well as the relationship of Indiana to the United States Constitution.

In the period before the Civil War, when the functions of the central government were extremely limited, the lives of Indiana residents were little affected by the United States Constitution and the power of the federal government. An important exception arose out of the jurisdiction over cases involving runaway slaves. The clause in the Constitution (Article IV, section 2) which declared: "No person held to service or labor in one State, under the laws thereof, escaping into another, shall in consequence of any law or regulation therein, be discharged from such service or labor, but shall be delivered up on claim of the party to whom such service or labor may be due," was an important source of friction in federal-state relations, as Patrick Furlong shows in his lecture on the South Bend Fugitive Slave Cases. Although the court decisions in the cases did not alter existing legal precedents, Furlong says: "Far more important is what these cases demonstrate in the matter of fundamental law, the inability of the American people by either political or judicial means to settle the great sectional conflict over slavery which was tearing the American union asunder." The cases illustrate the "dangers and difficulties which occur when moral imperatives conflict with legal duties."

Slavery, in particular the political issue of the expansion of slavery into the territories, was an important factor in the impasse between North and South which led to the Civil War, a conflict which challenged the supremacy of the Union and the United States Constitution. The problem which our nation faces in every war—how to achieve military victory without violating individual rights guaranteed by the Constitution—was more acute in this conflict, a war fought between Americans on American soil. As Alan Nolan says: "The response of the United States to the Southern rebellion took place within the general context of the legal system and without a suspension of the conventional political process. But there were impositions in the legal system and the political process." Arbitrary arrests and suspension of the writ of habeas corpus, used to cope with the problem of internal dissent and subversion, were justified in President Lincoln's view as necessary to uphold the Constitution and preserve the Union. In an oft quoted address he asked: "are all laws *but one* to go unexecuted and the government itself go to pieces, lest that one be violated?"

In the case with which Nolan is concerned, Lambdin P. Milligan of Huntington, Indiana, a civilian, was charged with treason, tried in a military court, and sentenced to be hanged. After the end of the war the United States Supreme Court ruled that the proceedings violated the Constitution, holding that the military lacked jurisdiction to try civilians so long as civil courts were open and functioning—a decision which Nolan calls "a curb of executive and military power," one long regarded as a landmark in the history of civil liberties.

The Thirteenth Amendment, adopted at the end of the Civil War, abolished slavery, but there remained the question of the status of the emancipated slaves and their descendants. The Fourteenth Amendment, ratified in 1868, granted them citizenship and prohibited a state from denying "any person within its jurisdiction the equal protection of the laws." Interpretation of the Equal Protection Clause became the central issue in countless court decisions involving racial segregation. The Indianapolis School Busing Case, begun in 1968, a century after the adoption of the Fourteenth Amendment, is a recent example. The case is constitutionally significant because of the criteria used to determine violation of "equal protection of the laws" and for the remedy which the court devised.

While much of the work of the United States Supreme Court in recent decades has dealt with the rights of minorities under the guarantees of the Fourteenth Amendment, perhaps of equal importance have been cases arising under the Bill of Rights and the First Amendment in particular. Two of the lectures in the series "Indiana and the United States Constitution" deal with First Amendment freedoms. In the Kinsey Customs Case Kenneth Stevens considers the question of obscenity. While the Supreme Court has consistently held that obscenity is not protected by the First Amendment guarantees of freedom of speech and press, it has never defined the term precisely. The Kinsey case, involving materials imported for research purposes by Alfred Kinsey of the Indiana University Institute for Sex Research, turned on the question of whether this constituted a violation of the Tariff Act of 1930, which prohibited the importation of obscene materials. A federal court ruled that scientists at the Institute had the right to import and study materials which, under ordinary circumstances, would be considered obscene. The decision helped to establish the concept of "variable obscenity" in censorship law—that obscenity is not absolute but varies according to the persons and uses involved. It marked a victory for freedom for scholarly research.

Irving Fink's lecture, "Bible Biology," involves the currently controversial issue of evolution *v.* creationism. Although tried in a local Indiana court, the case, dealing with an important constitutional question, attracted attention nationally.

Over a period of years the Supreme Court has held that the guarantees of the Bill of Rights are applicable to the states through the process of incorporating them into the clause of the Fourteenth Amendment which prohibits states from denying "liberty" without "due process of law." At issue in this case was the clause which says: "Congress shall make no law respecting an establishment of religion or prohibiting the free exercise thereof." A biology textbook prepared by the Textbook Committee of the Creation Research Society and approved by the Indiana State Commission on Textbook Adoptions had been adopted in some Indiana schools. The court found the book religiously sectarian in nature and hence an abridgement of the constitutional separation of church and state.

The final lecture, "Conceptualizing the Constitution," instead of focusing on a single case is more general in nature. In the words of David Papke it differs in significant ways from the earlier lectures—it "disdains extended historical narratives with conclusions" and instead "attempts to offer broad conceptualizations and examples." In the lecture Papke develops three concepts of the Constitution: as icon, as text, and as law. The idea of icon, an object of veneration, has a special appeal as the United States prepares to celebrate the Bicentennial of the Constitution.

Acknowledgments

The lectures and the publication of this book are the products of the efforts and support of a number of individuals and organizations. The lectures were made possible by a grant from the Indiana Committee for the Humanities which paid the honoraria and other costs. The History Department of Indiana University Indianapolis contributed office facilities and secretarial assistance. The Indiana Historical Bureau helped with planning and printing brochures and with publicity. The Indiana State Library contributed use of its auditorium. Receptions which afforded opportunity for informal discussions following the lectures were funded by a small grant from the Lincoln National Life Foundation, Inc., of Fort Wayne. Publication of this book is possible because of the generosity of the Indiana Historical Society.

Scholarly and thoughtful commentaries following the lectures enhanced their value and provided material for discussion. Commentators were: Professor Maurice Baxter of the History Department, Indiana University Bloomington; Mark Neely, Director, The Louis A. Warren Lincoln Library and Museum; Professor William Marsh of the Law School, Indiana University Indianapolis; Fay William, Indianapolis attorney; Dean Howard Mehlinger, School of Education, Indiana University; Professor James Madison of the History Department, Indiana University Bloomington.

In addition to officers of the Indiana Association of Historians the following persons served as moderators of three of the lectures: Professor Patrick Baude of the Law School, Indiana University Bloomington; James Farmer, Indianapolis newspaperman; and Victor Smith, Supervisor of Social Studies, Indianapolis Public Schools.

Members of the staff of the Indiana Historical Society gave valuable assistance in the presentation of the lectures as well as in the editing and publication of this book. Special thanks are due Gayle Thornbrough, Director of the Society until October 1985; Peter Harstad, present Director; Paula Corpuz and Kent Calder, editors; Kathy Breen, Paul Brockman, Leigh Darbee, Tom Krasean, Barbara McCurdy, Mary Ann Ponder, and Robert M. Taylor, Jr. Robert Barrows and Pamela Bennett of the Indiana Historical Bureau furnished suggestions and contributed valuable time.

Officers and a lecture committee of the Indiana Association of Historians planned the lectures and the book. They include Clifton Phillips of the History Department, DePauw University; Bernard Friedman of the History Department, Indiana University Indianapolis; Oakah Jones of the History Department, Purdue University; Robert M. Taylor, Jr., of the Indiana Historical Society; William Giffin of the History Department, Indiana State University; and Robert Barrows of the Indiana Historical Bureau. Emma Lou Thornbrough served as director of the lecture series, Bernard Friedman as co-director, and William Giffin as fiscal agent.

Emma Lou Thornbrough

The South Bend Fugitive Slave Case

Patrick J. Furlong

Mr. Furlong is Professor of History at Indiana University, South Bend. He is coauthor of "Schuyler Colfax: A Reputation Tarnished" in Gentlemen from Indiana: National Party Candidates, 1836-1940. *His book* Indiana: An Illustrated History *was published in 1985.*

The South Bend fugitive slave cases comprise one unnecessary application for a probably illegal warrant, four writs of habeas corpus, and scattered charges of riot, false imprisonment, and kidnapping, all in the courts of Indiana. In addition, there were federal actions for damages by a citizen of Kentucky against citizens of Indiana, settled in part by the Supreme Court of the United States. The entire proceedings required little more than two years, although there were derivative actions for slander and collection of damages which extended for another four years. The narrow legal questions raised by these cases are of great interest but of narrow importance, as the governing precedents were clear enough and not altered in the slightest by the decisions given here. Far more important is what these cases demonstrate in the matter of fundamental constitutional law, the inability of the American people by either political or judicial means to settle the great sectional conflict over slavery which was tearing the American union asunder.

David and Lucy Powell and their four sons were the property of John Norris of Boone County, Kentucky, whose farm was on the banks of the Ohio River not far from Lawrenceburg, Indiana. On Saturday night, October 9, 1847, the entire Powell family ran away to the free state of Indiana. Norris pursued them the next morning with a large search party, which found no trace of the fugitives although the search continued for two months.[1] By an unknown route and with unknown aid, the Powell family made its way to Cass County, in the southwestern part of Michigan, where there was already a substantial community of Negro residents, many of them runaway slaves.[2]

Two years later Norris somehow learned of the whereabouts of his missing slaves and traveled northward with a small party of friends to capture the fugitives and bring them back to Kentucky. Late on a Thursday night, September 27, 1849, Norris approached the Powells' isolated house in the woods, inquiring for strayed cattle. As soon as he recognized the fugitives, Norris loudly announced himself and his purpose, while his friends brandished pistols and bowie knives. Lucy Powell was roused from her sleep and "with threatening language and in a violent manner dragged . . . from her bed," tied with cords, and placed in a covered wagon. Her husband and one of the younger boys were away, but the three sons with her were also seized and placed in the wagon. Three other black men and a white farmer from the neighborhood were in the house, but they offered no resistance. An armed guard remained until daybreak to prevent them from giving the alarm, while Norris and the rest of the party began their journey to Kentucky.[3]

Friday morning Norris passed through South Bend without attracting attention. About noon Wright Maudlin, a white friend of the Powell family, reached South Bend in his pursuit of the wagon and raised the alarm. He was directed to a tough-minded lawyer who despised slavery, Edwin B. Crocker, and the two men quickly secured a writ of habeas corpus for the captives. The word spread rapidly among South Bend's 1,500 residents that "a gang of kidnappers [had] just gone through town with a lot of negroes that they had kidnapped over in Michigan." Maudlin, Crocker, a deputy sheriff, and a group of residents, both black and white, set off in pursuit. A mile or two from town they discovered Norris and his entire party, where they had pulled off the road to feed their horses. A crowd estimated at 15 to 20 by the defendants and at more than 140 by the plaintiffs gathered around the wagon as the deputy sheriff served the writ. Leander B. Newton made threatening remarks which prompted one of the Kentuckians to ask, "What riled that damned old fool?" Both sides were armed but there was no violence, and Norris agreed to return to South Bend where he was promised a fair trial in the case of the fugitives. The four members of the Powell family were placed in jail for safekeeping.[4]

John Norris kept his head, avoided any actions which might have further antagonized the hostile crowd, and soon acquired shrewd lawyers of his own, Jonathan A. Liston and Thomas S. Stanfield. The original nonspecific writ of habeas corpus was replaced with a new writ listing all four Powells by name and directed to Norris by name as well. After an hour or so to prepare their cases, the opposing lawyers appeared at the courthouse before Probate Judge Elisha Egbert. Under a statute passed earlier that year, St. Joseph County was added to the brief list of Indiana counties where the probate court was given concurrent jurisdiction with the circuit court in habeas corpus cases.[5]

Norris swore that Lucy, Lewis, George, and James Powell were all slaves, his rightful property under the laws of Kentucky. They had fled his service, and he had discovered them in the state of Michigan, arrested them there as fugitives from labor, and was returning with them to Kentucky. Edwin Crocker and Albert G. Deavitt for the fugitives answered that Norris's claim was "not sufficient in law" to justify his continued custody of the Powells. There was a long argument, apparently without reference to the precedents, as to whether the federal Fugitive Act of 1793 required or simply permitted a slaveholder to secure a judge's certificate authorizing the return of recaptured slaves to the state from which they had fled. Norris admitted that he had not taken the trouble to obtain such a certificate, either in Michigan or in Indiana. The hearing continued into the night, and Judge Egbert ruled that Norris had not met the requirements of the Fugitive Act and ordered the Powells released from custody.[6]

A large crowd had waited quietly throughout the hearing. In anticipation of the judge's ruling, Liston advised Norris to obtain a warrant to arrest the Powells as fugitives from labor under the Indiana fugitive law of 1824, and this he did. Judge Egbert pronounced his decision releasing the fugitives in a low voice, but Crocker shouted three times to the crowd that they were free. Norris took off his hat and pulled out the freshly issued fugitive warrant which he tried to read above the noise of the hostile crowd. He could not make himself heard and pushed across the courtroom to Lucy Powell, grabbed her with one arm, and drew his pistol with the other. The Kentuckians surrounded the Powells, who remained seated on a bench, and flourished their pistols and bowie knives at the outraged crowd. Liston jumped on a table and shouted to the Kentuckians, "Gentlemen, protect your property!" Then this fine lawyer added, "The first man that touches your property, blow them through!" Amable La Pierre shouted to the Kentuckians to put away their weapons, and one of them shouted back: "God damn your soul, what are you talking about weapons for, standing there with a club in your hands." Judge Egbert had not adjourned the court, but he must have been too shocked to cite anyone for contempt. Some of the bystanders removed the sash from a window and tried to push a black man through the opening, but he cried out that he was free and did not need to be rescued. No one was injured, and Sheriff Lot Day and

Norris agreed that the fugitives should be kept in jail until Monday morning when there would be further legal arguments. Edwin Crocker, the leading lawyer for the fugitives, went inside the jail to confer with the sheriff and emerged after a few moments to assure the crowd that they would not be returned to Kentucky without a fair trial. Calm returned to the streets of South Bend, but the legal dispute became only more complicated.[7]

On Friday evening and Saturday morning warrants were sworn and served on Norris and his five companions, charging them with assault, battery, and riot as a result of the uproar in the courthouse. The riot accusation was made by Leander B. Newton. Lewis Powell, the eldest of the Powell sons, petitioned for a new writ of habeas corpus, directed against the sheriff, and it was issued for a return on Monday morning. Like all of the actions filed by members of the Powell family, it was in the handwriting of Edwin B. Crocker. Before he finished his work on Friday evening, Crocker also managed to write out and file two civil actions against Norris, one on behalf of David and Lucy Powell and the other for Lewis Powell, both charging false imprisonment. The Kentuckians spent much of the day Saturday defending themselves before the local justice of the peace, and on the felony riot charge they were held for the circuit court term which opened the following Monday, October 1. During the day on Saturday a large number of Negroes from Michigan joined local residents on the streets, and many people were seen carrying clubs while a smaller number, both white and black, were armed with more deadly weapons. The blacks were variously estimated to number between fifty and four hundred, and they remained until Monday morning to see the result of the second trial.[8]

Edwin B. Crocker used a variety of tricks to prevent Norris from regaining control of the fugitives over the weekend. First he tried and failed to persuade the circuit court clerk to refuse the fugitive warrant which Norris sought on Friday evening. He gave as justification the unconstitutionality of the Indiana fugitive law, but instead of citing a specific case he referred the clerk to the retired circuit judge, Samuel C. Sample. Crocker probably had the 1842 case of *Prigg* v. *Pennsylvania* in mind, but he was without the proper reference and telegraphed to a friend in nearby Niles, Michigan, for the appropriate volume of *Peters Reports*.[9] Wright Maudlin returned to Michigan and filed kidnapping charges against Norris, and Crocker gave the fugitive warrant to the constable on Saturday evening, instructing him not to serve it unless Norris and his companions attempted to leave town before Monday. Crocker's excuse was the need to wait for the arrival of a Michigan lawyer who never reached South Bend, and the warrant remained unserved in the hands of the constable until it was returned to Crocker sometime Monday. Crocker personally warned the sheriff not to release the fugitives to Norris, citing the third habeas corpus writ as his authority.[10]

Sunday passed quietly and without public disturbance, although both Liston for the slave owner and Crocker for the fugitives were busy laying traps for one another. Norris spent much of the day trying to persuade the people of South Bend that he was a kind and considerate master. He said that he had never whipped his slaves and allowed them to keep a boat so they could cross over to Indiana to sell their garden produce whenever they pleased. When the sheriff refused Norris's demand to hand over the fugitives under the state warrant he had secured, the Kentucky slave owner gave up any hope of regaining his slaves. In consultation with his attorney, Norris decided instead to seek his remedy in the more friendly confines of the federal courts. Crocker said afterward that Norris and Liston hoped to entrap him in some violation of the law, but he refused to assume any personal responsibility for the fugitives. Crocker carefully arranged for two witnesses to hear his conversation with the sheriff on the question of custody of the fugitives. Liston asked Crocker several times why he refused to serve the warrant naming Norris as a fugitive from justice on the Michigan kidnapping charge, but Crocker evaded the question because he suspected that Liston would use Norris's arrest as his own excuse for declining to present evidence at the habeas corpus hearing scheduled for Monday morning.[11]

Early that next morning Liston and Crocker confronted one another in the office of the court clerk. As the clerk remembered their remarks, Crocker challenged Liston to present his evidence, if he had any, and prove that the fugitives were rightfully the property of John Norris. Crocker claimed that he would be able to prove that they were free. The clerk's memory was not precise enough for the lawyers who took his deposition, but Liston apparently told Crocker that he would be held personally to account for rescuing the fugitives. Judge Egbert was also present, and his memory was also faulty, although he did remember hearing Crocker say that he was ready for trial, with witnesses who would prove that the Powells were legally free. "You have rescued the slaves from Norris," Liston told Crocker, "and you begin to dread the consequences, and you would like Norris to appear and make a fool of himself and let you out of the difficulty."[12]

When Judge Egbert opened the probate court about nine o'clock, Sheriff Lot Day appeared with the four Negroes to answer the writ of habeas corpus. Norris was summoned, but neither he nor his attorneys appeared, and as Norris's fugitive warrant was the sheriff's only authority for holding the Powell family, the judge heard their evidence and ordered them released. As Crocker described the touching scene:

> The colored friends and neighbors of the captives immediately came forward, conducted them out of the court-house to a wagon, and quietly rode off home with them. On the bridge adjacent to town, they halted, and made the welkin ring with their cheers for liberty. They rode off, singing the songs of freedom, rejoicing over the fortunate escape of their friends from the horrible fate of slavery.[13]

Norris and his Kentucky associates stood quietly along the street and watched the fugitives depart and then attended to their own legal difficulties. With the fugitives safely back in Michigan the grand jurors of St. Joseph County had no further interest in the Kentuckians, and they declined to indict them on the charge of riot. A fourth and final writ of habeas corpus, prepared by Edwin B. Crocker on behalf of Lewis Powell, was served against John Norris. In his last appearance before the St. Joseph Probate Court, Norris calmly swore that he did not have the person named in his custody, and that was the end of the matter.[14]

Or so it seemed to the residents of South Bend. Norris and his friends returned to Kentucky, the Powells returned to Michigan, and presumably some of the lawyers collected their fees. Norris was true to his word and sued for damages in federal court; for however strange it may seem to modern ideas of fairness and due process, every action that Norris took to regain his property was strictly legal, and those who stood in his way made themselves liable for penalties under section four of the federal Fugitive Act.[15]

Just what was the law of the land respecting fugitives from labor in the year 1849? The relevant statute was the Fugitive Act of 1793, which dealt with fugitives from justice in sections one and two and with fugitives from labor in sections three and four. The law was enacted by overwhelming majorities in both House and Senate in response to a criminal extradition dispute between Pennsylvania and Virginia, and for many years the fugitive slave provisions operated without difficulty. The law afforded no protection for fugitive slaves. They could be arrested without warrant and returned to labor without formal process, and if there was process, it was by summary judgment. In theory the fugitive from labor was treated in the same way as a fugitive from justice, and the purpose of the federal law was to return the fugitive to state jurisdiction, for trial or for labor. If a person of color claimed that he was held unlawfully as a slave, his legal remedy was through the state courts. That this remedy existed in theory but not in practice did not trouble those who framed and interpreted the federal law.[16]

The legal principle that slavery depended upon positive law and could not exist where it was not explicitly supported by statute was familiar to every lawyer in Britain and America.[17] The difficulty was that certain states of the American union favored and supported slavery while others did not, and the question which came before federal courts was the degree of protection that should be afforded to slave property in states which did not recognize slavery. With a substantial record of consistency over a period of half a century, federal judges upheld the rights of slave owners and ignored the plight of free persons of color who might have been claimed as slaves. They ignored as well the sovereign rights of those states which chose not to aid slave owners in pursuit of runaway slaves. From *Bell* v. *Hogan* in 1811, federal judges adhered to the principle that in any claim for freedom "it is incumbent upon the negro to show that he is free. . . ." In the absence of clear evidence to the contrary, any person of color living in or traveling from a slave state was presumed to be a slave.[18]

The constitutionality of the 1793 statute was repeatedly upheld, and those who obstructed efforts to recapture fugitive slaves were punished for their violation of the law. In a case from the District of Columbia the circuit court reaffirmed that "every negro is, by a rule of evidence well established in this part of the country, prima facie to be considered as a slave, and the property of somebody. . . ." A stagecoach line was held liable for aiding an escape because its agent sold a ticket to a runaway slave for the trip from Washington to Baltimore.[19]

In an 1833 case concerning the arrest of a fugitive slave in Pennsylvania over the objections of a considerable crowd of Quakers and other opponents of slavery, Justice Henry Baldwin emphasized the legality of slavery and the importance of obedience to law. To indulge in "humane and benevolent feelings" in violation of the law would infringe the rights of property owners and weaken the rule of law so essential to society. Such unlawful opposition to slavery, Baldwin warned, was "false philanthropy which prostrates the law and the constitution. . . ." The federal circuit court in New York ruled that no warrant or other legal process was required for the arrest of a fugitive slave. The only proper role for the magistrate was to sanction the removal of the fugitive to the state where the person claiming his labor resided, and this matter of law did not require a trial by jury. This principle was reaffirmed with even greater emphasis in an 1851 case from Massachusetts where the court ruled that return of a fugitive slave was precisely similar to the extradition of an accused criminal, a matter to be decided without a jury:

> The certificate, of itself, gives no authority whatever to treat the party as a slave. It is merely a warrant to remove him to a certain place. If . . . the claimant exacts service, he must find his justification . . . in the laws of the state where the service is required.

Judge Peleg Sprague reminded his New England friends that the Fugitive Act had been supported by distinguished New England members of Congress and passed at a time when many in Congress had attended the Constitutional Convention. "And it was not until years afterwards," Sprague continued, "when a new generation had arisen, that its constitutionality was questioned." Since the ratification of the Constitution "we of Massachusetts and the North have undergone a change, but this cannot alter pre-existing facts."[20]

The most celebrated fugitive slave case was *Prigg* v. *Pennsylvania*, a widely cited case decided by the Supreme Court in 1842. Edwin B. Crocker relied upon this case in arguing that the Indiana law respecting fugitive slaves was unconstitutional. Edward Prigg was sent from Maryland into Pennsylvania in pursuit of a fugitive slave, and he was arrested, tried, and convicted under a Pennsylvania law which made it illegal to remove a Negro from the state by force with the intention of returning him to slavery. The law did provide for the return of fugitives under proper state warrants and after a hearing before a judge, and except for proceeding under this law, Pennsylvania judges were forbidden to act under the federal Fugitive Law of 1793. Prigg, as it happened, had not followed the prescribed procedure under the federal or the state law. The state of Maryland, arguing for Prigg, held that Article IV of the Constitution gave to Congress exclusive power to legislate in fugitive slave matters. Justice Joseph Story of Massachusetts wrote the court's opinion holding the Pennsylvania law to be unconstitutional. The Constitution, Story wrote,

> manifestly contemplates the existence of a positive, unqualified right on the part of the owner of the slave, which no State law or regulation can in any way qualify, regulate, control, or restrain.

Northern states lacked even the power to delay the recapture of a fugitive from labor:

> The owner must . . . have the right to seize and repossess the slave, which the local laws of his own State confer upon him as property; and we all know that the right of seizure and recaption is universally acknowledged in all the slaveholding States.

Slave owners had the right to take fugitive slaves anywhere in the Union, and this right derived from the Constitution itself and did not depend upon statutory support. The federal statute of 1793 merely provided a more practical method for the return of fugitives, and it superseded all state laws on the subject. Justice Story admitted some doubts about the power of Congress to authorize state judges to act under a federal law, but this question was not at issue in the Prigg case. "Under the Constitution," Story concluded, the recapture of fugitive slaves "is recognized as an absolute, positive right and duty, pervading the whole Union with an equal and supreme force, uncontrolled and uncontrollable by state sovereignty or state legislation." Such was the law of the land as interpreted by the Supreme Court, and the possibility that under this law free blacks might be claimed as slaves, a point argued by Pennsylvania before the court, was simply ignored.[21]

Antislavery lawyers tried unsuccessfully to argue around the Prigg decision, but the judges were highly unsympathetic. The most notable effort was *Jones* v. *Van Zandt*, an Ohio case on a charge of harboring a fugitive slave which was decided by the Supreme Court in 1847. Salmon P. Chase, who would become Chief Justice of the United States in 1864, published his brief for the defense in a pamphlet which ran to 108 pages. His arguments were eloquent and involved, as were those of his distinguished colleague William H. Seward, but to no effect. The justices unanimously upheld the validity of the Fugitive Act of 1793 and rejected all of Chase and Seward's efforts to explain why transporting a suspicious black person in a covered wagon was not concealing and harboring a fugitive.[22]

In another northwestern state the following year there was a case similar in many ways to the happenings in South Bend. A crowd of antislavery men in Marshall, Michigan, rescued six fugitives from their master, who filed suit to recover damages for his loss. In his charge to the jury, Justice John McLean read the law plainly: "Where the slave absconds, the master may reclaim him."[23]

Indiana legislators and judges had attempted to deal with the problem of fugitive slaves since territorial days, but the problem defied solution. The first law on the subject passed in 1810 and provided that persons claiming a fugitive must appear before a judge and prove legal ownership before the fugitive could be removed from the territory. At the first session of the state legislature in 1816, Gov. Jonathan Jennings asked for a more effective measure to restrain unlawful captures while providing for the orderly return of properly identified fugitives. The legislature responded with "An Act to Prevent Manstealing," which again provided that no fugitive could be taken from Indiana without a certificate issued by a judge after a jury trial upon the merits of the slave owner's claim. Furthermore, the fugitive was to be arrested by the sheriff upon a proper warrant and not by the slave owner himself. These provisions were in clear conflict with federal law, as Judge Benjamin Parke ruled two years later in the first fugitive slave case from Indiana to reach the federal courts.[24]

There were a number of cases which led to the exchange of unpleasant letters between the governors of Indiana and Kentucky, but not until 1824 did the legislature adopt a new fugitive law. The procedure adopted in 1824 provided significantly less protection for the fugitive, although slave owners were still required to obtain a warrant before arresting a fugitive and to take their prisoners before a judge for a summary hearing. There are no reported state cases involving fugitive slaves until 1849, when the Indiana Supreme Court ruled the state's 1824 fugitive law unconstitutional by virtue of the U.S. Supreme Court's decision in *Prigg* v. *Pennsylvania*. None of the lawyers in South Bend seem to have been aware of this case, although it came on an appeal from neighboring Elkhart County and was decided in May of 1849.[25]

Also ignorant of the law was the intensely political editor of the only newspaper in South Bend. Schuyler Colfax opposed slavery, but he was more moderate on the subject than most Whigs in the northern states. Colfax himself was threatened with a lawsuit for his one article on the fugitive case in South Bend, and he became uncomfortably aware that federal law favored the slave owners. Colfax maintained that a black, "accused" of slavery as he put it, should be presumed free just as a person accused of crime was presumed innocent, and the case properly tried by judge and jury. These may have been noble sentiments, but the law was otherwise.[26]

John Norris had lost four of his slaves beyond any hope of recovery, but he did not intend to bear the financial hardship from his own resources. Three months after leaving South Bend he filed suit in the United States Circuit Court for the District of Indiana against nine defendants. The first named was the obnoxious bystander who had charged Norris with riot, Leander B. Newton, and the case was styled *Norris* v. *Newton et al.* Wright Maudlin, who had been the first to aid the fugitives, escaped because he was a resident of Michigan, not Indiana as the suit charged; but Lot Day, the sheriff who had refused to hand over the fugitives, and Edwin B. Crocker, the attorney who had filed so many motions on their behalf, had to face the accusation of harboring fugitive slaves and aiding in their escape. Section four of the Fugitive Act of 1793 provided a penalty of $500 for any person who obstructed or hindered anyone lawfully claiming a fugitive slave, or who concealed, harbored, or rescued the fugitive.[27] Norris would have his revenge and his money, and the law made his victory almost certain.

The case was tried at Indianapolis in May, 1850, with District Judge Elisha M. Huntington and circuit-riding Justice John McLean jointly presiding. The facts of the case were clear and beyond significant dispute, and the arguments were on the application of the law. Jonathan Liston appeared for Norris, while two of Crocker's associates represented the defendants. More than forty witnesses were summoned, and additional evidence was presented by deposition. The defense relied chiefly on the existence of the writs of habeas corpus to excuse their harboring of the fugitives, but to no avail. While the circuit court was sitting in Indianapolis, Gov. John Jordan Crittenden of Kentucky paid an official visit upon Gov. Joseph A. Wright of Indiana, and Crittenden used the occasion to speak on the importance of sectional harmony and the duty of Hoosiers to return slaves who had fled from their owners in Kentucky. Crocker claimed that Crittenden's address, which was heard by the jurors, prejudiced the case against him.[28]

Far more damaging for the defendants was Justice McLean's lengthy charge to the jury. After reviewing the events in South Bend, McLean expounded the law. He explained that a master had a right to seize a runaway slave wherever he might be found and take him back to slavery "without any exhibition of claim, or authority," as long as this could be accomplished without a breach of the peace. A state judge indeed had a right to issue a writ of habeas corpus upon a properly sworn application. As McLean explained, "There can be no higher offense against the laws of humanity and justice, or against the dignity of a state and its laws, than to arrest a freeman within its protection, with a view of making him a slave." If Norris had taken the fugitives before a judge in Michigan and proceeded according to section three of the Fugitive Act there would have been no problem, but his failure to do so did not in any way lessen his legal custody of them in Indiana. The writ of habeas corpus was issued and served, and Norris duly appeared before the court and justified his custody of the fugitives, and that should have been an end to the matter. Judge Egbert had ruled otherwise, but his ruling was wrong and of no effect, and so as McLean explained to the jurors:

> Every step taken subsequently was against law and in violation of his [Norris's] rights. I deem it unnecessary to inquire into the procedure subsequently. It was wholly without authority. The forms of law assumed afford no protection to any one. The slaves were taken from the legal custody of their master, and he thereby lost their services.

Crocker was not liable for any advice he had given as counsel to the slaves, but for any actions exceeding the proper duty of a lawyer he was of course responsible. Justice McLean concluded with some final remarks on the duty of jurors to try the case according to the law rather than their private consciences:

> We must stand by the law. We have sworn to maintain it. It is expected that the citizens of the free states should be opposed to slavery. But with the abstract principles of slavery we have nothing to do . . . . Our duty is found in the constitution of the Union, as construed by the supreme court. The fugitives from labor we are bound, by the highest obligations, to deliver up on claim of the master . . . and there is no state power which can release the slave from the legal custody of his master.

After listening to such instructions from an associate justice of the Supreme Court, it should not be surprising that the jury found in favor of Norris and awarded damages of $2,856.[29]

South Bend had not heard its final blast from John Norris of Boone County, Kentucky, for after winning his case at Indianapolis he directed Liston to file suits against fifteen additional defendants, and rumor had it that twenty-five more victims might be named later. The suits were filed between June 29 and October 3, but on September 18 the Fugitive Slave Act of 1850 became law, and Norris's prospects suddenly became far more complicated. Among the new defendants was Judge Egbert, although the precise accusation against him is not known. Egbert was linked in the case with an additional suit against Crocker, and the action was styled *Norris* v. *Crocker and Egbert*.[30]

The second federal trial opened at Indianapolis in November, 1850, and the dispute now centered about the conflict between section four of the 1793 statute and section seven of the new Fugitive Slave Act, which set forth differing provisions for penalties. The question was argued for two days, and the court put off its decision until the May term. A decision was then given for the defendants, but in order to permit an appeal the two judges certified a *pro forma* difference of opinion which permitted the case to go to the Supreme Court. There the defense was entrusted to the distinguished abolitionist lawyer Salmon P. Chase, while the plaintiff continued with his Indiana attorney, former senator Oliver H. Smith. The arguments in Washington in December of 1851 concerned narrow legal questions of conflict of statutes, implicit repeal, and the effect of a repeal upon actions pending under the old statute. Under the 1793 law the owner was permitted to sue for the penalty against those who aided the fugitive, while under the new law the penalty was made criminal and the prosecution was at the instance of the United States Attorney. The Supreme Court held unanimously that the 1850 Fugitive Slave Act had indeed repealed the penalty clause of the 1793 Fugitive Act, and as plaintiff's right to recover damages depended exclusively upon the repealed portion of the law, all further proceedings in the matter were barred.[31] Norris would be able to recover no further damages from the people of South Bend who had rescued his fugitive slaves.

The antislavery zealots of South Bend paid dearly for their principles. Liston was aggressive in collecting the damages awarded Norris, and he managed to extort money from others merely by threatening to sue. The surviving records do not show how much each defendant paid, but one was allowed to settle for as little as $20, while another paid $1,000, and several had to pay $200 each. Little wonder that a Whig editor like Schuyler Colfax expressed sympathy for the defendants and their "pecuniary prostration." The verdict was indeed a heavy one for what Colfax regarded as "an indiscretion . . . an excess of zeal in favor of Freedom." The real and personal property of some of the defendants was sold by the United States marshal, and when sympathetic fellow citizens refused to bid, Liston bought several parcels of real estate in the name of John Norris.[32]

Norris also pursued Edwin B. Crocker with a vengeance, suing him twice for aiding the fugitives, and then suing him again for slander in saying "you kidnapped negroes and I will have you in the penitentiary." Crocker moved to California in 1852 where he enjoyed a distinguished career leading to chief justice of the state. Leander B. Newton returned to his obscurity as a local brickmason. Another of the defendants, Amable La Pierre, attempted to evade payment of damages by a fraudulent conveyance of his real estate, and in September, 1851, Norris filed an action in chancery before the federal court. La Pierre and nine others, along with the State Bank of Indiana, were the defendants, and Leander B. Newton and Edwin B. Crocker were naturally among the group. *Norris v. La Pierre et al.* was decided in December, 1854, in Norris's favor of course, and the plaintiff was awarded damages and costs of $5,756. There was another sale of property in South Bend at the hands of the United

States marshal in 1855, and Norris collected at least $5,192 as his final compensation for one woman, one young man, and two teenage boys rescued from slavery by the bench, bar, and populace of South Bend, in open defiance of the laws of the United States.[33]

What can the South Bend Fugitive Slave Cases tell us about the Constitution and its place in American life? The clearest lessons, warnings perhaps, are the dangers and difficulties which occur when moral imperatives conflict with legal duties. As Justice McLean charged the jurors in Indianapolis in May of 1850:

> Society has a claim upon all its citizens. General rules have been adopted, in the form of laws, for the protection of the rights of persons and things. These laws lie at the foundation of the social compact, and their observance is essential to the maintenance of civilization. In these matters, the law, and not conscience, constitutes the rule of action . . . . What may be deemed a conscientious act by one individual, may be held criminal by another.[34]

True enough, and what else would one expect a judge to say. But in certain exceptional matters, with full regard for the risks and in full readiness to accept the consequences, conscience must prevail even over the law. To deny this would be to deny the American Revolution itself, and we would all have to return to the study of the British Constitution.

Was slavery so terrible a wrong that the rule of law, the Constitution, the American Union itself should be overthrown? There were those in the North who answered that the Constitution was in league with the devil and should be abandoned at once, while many others, both in the North and in the South, sought a peaceful and gradual remedy. In the end the Union was preserved, the Constitution was reinterpreted and amended, slavery was abolished, and 618,000 Americans died because their fellow citizens could find no way short of civil war to settle the constitutional differences which first hit home to the people of South Bend in 1849. What Northerners called freedom, Southerners insisted was the theft of their property. Federal law and federal judges upheld slavery, as did the Constitution itself, and thus was the moral issue denied. But conscience refused to allow the immorality of human slavery to be denied. For as Schuyler Colfax gave his editorial benediction over the defendants in 1849:

Though human Courts may award verdicts and mulct them in damages—we hold them guiltless of any offense against the great Laws of
Humanity or the greater Laws of God.[35]

The Constitution may be the last word for lawyers and jurists, but
for the people as a whole there is on rare and special occasions a
higher law which in the fullness of time perhaps becomes part of an
amended and improved Constitution. We should indeed cherish the
Constitution, but we should never forget that it is written on parch-
ment and not in tablets of stone.

Notes

1. *The South Bend Fugitive Slave Case* (New York, 1851), 1. This anonymous pamphlet offered
for sale "at the Anti-Slavery Office" was almost certainly written by Edwin B. Crocker, a
South Bend lawyer who was a leading participant in the cases; *Norris* v. *Newton et al.* (Circuit
Court, District of Indiana, 1850), 18 Federal Cases 322, No. 10,307.

2. James O. Wheeler and Stanley D. Brunn, "Negro Migration into Rural Southwestern
Michigan," *Geographical Review* 58 (1968): 214–30.

3. Deposition of William Southwick, May 1, 1850, in unnumbered case file for *Norris* v.
Newton et al. in Papers of the U.S. Circuit Court for the District of Indiana, Record Group 21,
Regional Archives and Record Center, Chicago (hereafter cited as Case File). Lucy Powell's
affidavit of September 28, 1849, from the certified copy in the deposition of John T. Lindsey,
Clerk of the St. Joseph Circuit Court, February 13, 1850, Case File. A delayed and much
subdued account appeared in South Bend's only newspaper, the *St. Joseph Valley Register*,
October 18, 1849.

4. Depositions of Deputy Sheriff Russell Day, February 2, 1850, and George Frasier,
February 12, 1850, Case File; *Norris* v. *Newton* at 323; *Fugitive Slave Case*, 2–3; *St. Joseph Valley
Register*, October 18, 1849.

5. The Indiana habeas corpus statute can be found in *1843 Revised Statutes*, chap. 48. The
law giving the Probate Court of St. Joseph County habeas corpus jurisdiction passed on
January 10, 1849, *1849 Acts*, 71. See also depositions of Lindsey and Joseph Haney, March 1,
1850, Case File.

6. *Norris* v. *Newton* at 323; *Fugitive Slave Case*, 4–5; Lindsey deposition, Case File; *St. Joseph
Valley Register*, October 18, 1849. The Probate Order Book has no record of the habeas corpus
hearing, with no entries between the close of the August term on August 29 to the beginning
of the next term on November 19, 1849.

7. *Norris* v. *Newton* at 323; *Fugitive Slave Case*, 4–5; depositions of Haney and Lindsey, and
also of Michael De Camp, Abraham R. Harper, and Jacob Roof, all May 28, 1850, Case File;
St. Joseph Valley Register, October 18, 1849. The Kentuckians' view of the affair is given in an
unsigned letter published in the *Louisville Democrat*, quoted in the *St. Joseph Valley Register*,
October 25, 1849. Judge Egbert gave a deposition about what he saw in the courtroom, but
he was not asked to comment about the reasons for his decision. A day or two later he said to
various people about town that had he expected trouble he would have appointed additional
bailiffs to maintain order. Deposition of February 5–7, 1850, Case File.

8. *Norris* v. *Newton* at 324; *Fugitive Slave Case*, 5; depositions of Lindsey and Harper, and also

Charles M. Heaton and Portage Township Constable Charles A. Chandonai, both April 12, 1850, Case File; *St. Joseph Valley Register*, October 18, 1849, ignored the events of Saturday.

9. Lindsey and Heaton depositions, Case File.

10. Depositions of Chandonai, and also Noah Van Minkle and Daniel W. Earl, both February 11, 1850, Case File.

11. Depositions of Benjamin Wall and Daniel Schank, both January 30, 1850, Case File; *Fugitive Slave Case*, 6–7.

12. Lindsey deposition, March 5, 9, 26, 27, 1850, and also Egbert deposition, Case File.

13. *Fugitive Slave Case*, 7–8; Lindsey deposition, Case File; *St. Joseph Valley Register*, October 18, 25, 1849; *Norris* v. *Newton* at 324.

14. Lindsey deposition, and also deposition of Alpheus Thornton, February 1, 1850, Case File; *Norris* v. *Newton* at 324; *St. Joseph Valley Register*, October 25, 1849. The two civil actions for false imprisonment came before the circuit court on October 3 and were continued at the request of plantiffs' attorney. St. Joseph Circuit Court, Order Book 6, 244–45.

15. *Norris* v. *Newton* at 324; 1 *Statutes at Large* 302; *St. Joseph Valley Register*, October 25, 1849.

16. 1 *Statutes at Large* 302; the history of fugitive slave legislation and disputes is thoroughly and ably reviewed in Thomas D. Morris, *Free Men All: The Personal Liberty Laws of the North, 1780–1861* (Baltimore: Johns Hopkins University Press, 1974), and more briefly in Don E. Fehrenbacher, *The Dred Scott Case: Its Significance in American Law and Politics* (New York: Oxford University Press, 1978), 40–42. For an analysis of the conflict between state and federal jurisdiction see "American Slavery and the Conflict of Laws," *Columbia Law Review* 71 (1971), 74.

17. *The Case of James Sommersett, a Negro*, 20 Howell's State Trials (King's Bench, 1773), 1, at 82, where Chief Justice Lord Mansfield said that slavery "is so odious, that nothing can be suffered to support it, but positive law."

18. *Bell* v. *Hogan*, 3 Federal Cases 107, No. 1,253. The legality of both the 1793 and 1850 statutes was ably defended by Allen Johnson, "The Constitutionality of the Fugitive Slave Acts," *Yale Law Journal* 31 (1921), 161.

19. *Hill* v. *Low*, 12 Federal Cases 172, No. 6,494; *Mandeville et al.* v. *Cookenderfer*, 16 Federal Cases 580, Nos. 9,009 and 9,010.

20. *Johnson* v. *Tompkins et al.*, 13 Federal Cases 840, No. 7,416; *In re Martin*, 16 Federal Cases 881, No. 9,154; *U.S.* v. *Scott*, 27 Federal Cases 990, No. 16,240b.

21. *Prigg* v. *Pennsylvania*, 16 Peters [41 U.S.] 539, especially at 611, and at 622; the significance of this case is explained clearly by Fehrenbacher, *Dred Scott Case*, 43–47.

22. Salmon P. Chase, *Reclamation of Fugitives from Service* (Cincinnati: R. P. Donogh, 1847); *Jones* v. *Van Zandt*, 5 Howard [46 U.S.] 215. In *Driskell* v. *Parish*, 7 Federal Cases 1093, Nos. 4,087, 4,088, and 4,089 (1847, 1849, 1845), also from Ohio, Chase made similar arguments with a similar lack of success.

23. *Giltner* v. *Gorham et al.*, 10 Federal Cases 424, No. 5,453 (1848).

24. *In re Susan*, 23 Federal Cases 444, No. 13,632; Emma Lou Thornbrough, "Indiana and Fugitive Slave Legislation," *Indiana Magazine of History* 50 (September 1954): 201–6, provides a thorough account of Indiana's troubles with the fugitive slave question.

25. Thornbrough, "Indiana and Fugitive Slave Legislation," 209–17; the two statutes may be found in *Laws of the Indiana Territory* 138 and *1824 Acts* 221; for the continuation of the 1824 statute see also *1843 Revised Statutes* 1032; 1–8 Blackford's *passim* have no fugitive slave cases; *Graves and others* v. *The State*, 1 Indiana 368. In *Donnell* v. *The State*, 3 Indiana 480 (1852), the Indiana Supreme Court again declared the 1824 fugitive law unconstitutional, citing *Prigg* v. *Pennsylvania* but not its own decision three years earlier in *Graves and others* v. *The State*.

26. *St. Joseph Valley Register*, December 27, 1849; the most thorough judicial commentary on the legality and constitutionality of the fugitive slave laws is Justice Samuel Nelson's

charge to the grand jury for the U. S. Circuit Court for the southern district of New York in April, 1851, in 30 Federal Cases 1007, No. 18,261.

27. 1 *Statutes at Large* 302, at 305; *Fugitive Slave Case*, 9; *St. Joseph Valley Register*, December 27, 1849.

28. *Fugitive Slave Case*, 9–15.

29. *Norris* v. *Newton* at 324–326. The jury brought in its verdict on June 12, 1850, and the judgment was entered on June 14. U.S. Circuit Court, District of Indiana, Order Book D, 395, 399, Record Group 21, Regional Archives and Record Center, Chicago.

30. Summonses and related documents, Case File; *Fugitive Slave Case*, 22.

31. 9 *Statutes at Large* 462; *Fugitive Slave Case*, 22–23; *Norris* v. *Crocker and Egbert*, 13 Howard [54 U.S.] 429. The case was argued on November 21–22, 1850, and the disagreement between the two judges announced on May 31, 1851. The case was formally dismissed by the circuit court on November 20, 1852, at which time the other suits filed by Norris were also dismissed. Order Book D, 409, 438, 441, 448; Order Book E, 53, 273, Record Group 21, Regional Archives, Chicago.

32. Writs for seizure of property, June 27, December 23, 1850; marshal's return, November 18, 1850; answer to bill of complaint, November 6, 1851, all in Case File. Liston tried to collect $40 from Joseph Haney in August, 1850, as his share of the judgment. Haney, who was a carpenter, offered to pay $20 in services. Deposition of Joseph Haney, January 20–21, 1851, Case File. John Veasey denied any part in aiding the fugitives, but when Liston threatened to sue he agreed to pay $200, partly by assuming a note and partly by building a wagon for Liston. Deposition of John M. Veasey, January 20–21, 1851, Case File. For Colfax's comments see *St. Joseph Valley Register*, June 20, 1850.

33. On the slander suit see summons, June 29, 1850, and amended declaration, May 30, 1851, in Case File; for dismissal of suit see Order Book E, 234. For *Norris* v. *La Pierre et al*. see Order Book F, 74–77; and also summons, September 17, 1851, writ for sale of property, July 18, 1855, and marshal's memorandum of costs, June 8, 1855, Case File.

34. *Norris* v. *Newton* at 326.

35. Peter J. Riga, "The American Crisis over Slavery: An Example of the Relationship between Legality and Morality," *American Journal of Jurisprudence* 26 (1981):80; *St. Joseph Valley Register*, December 27, 1849. Many Northern states actively opposed the Fugitive Slave Act of 1850 by both legislative and judicial action, but Indiana accepted the law without official resistance. See Thornbrough, "Indiana and Fugitive Slave Legislation," 220–28, and Morris, *Free Men All*, 148–218. The Supreme Court devastated Wisconsin's efforts to resist the Fugitive Slave Act in *Abelman* v. *Booth*, 21 Howard [62 U.S.] 506 (1859), the last significant fugitive slave case to come before the court.

Two books which consider the legal, political, and moral problems of American slavery in the nineteenth century are Robert M. Cover, *Justice Accused: Antislavery and the Judicial Process* (New Haven: Yale University Press, 1975), and Paul Finkelman, *An Imperfect Union: Slavery, Federalism, and Comity* (Chapel Hill: University of North Carolina Press, 1981), a close study of the changing relationships between northern and southern states and the federal government on the slavery question.

Ex Parte Milligan: A Curb of Executive and Military Power

Alan T. Nolan

Mr. Nolan is an Indianapolis lawyer, partner in the firm of Ice Miller Donadio & Ryan. He is the author of The Iron Brigade, *a Civil War history, and* As Sounding Brass, *a contemporary novel.*

E x parte Milligan, the 1866 decision of the United States Supreme Court, is a chapter in the long story of the American Civil War. The response of the United States to the Southern rebellion took place within the general context of the legal system and without a suspension of the conventional political process. But there were impositions on the legal system and the political process, and the prosecution of Lambdin P. Milligan was such an imposition.

To state the case of *Ex parte Milligan* in a lawyer-like way is a relatively simple task, but the political context of the case is essential to an appreciation of its significance. A consideration of the political context also permits an inquiry into the question of Indiana's role in the Civil War.

Abraham Lincoln

On March 4, 1861, Abraham Lincoln stood on a temporary platform on the east front of the unfinished Capitol in Washington. Following an introduction by his friend Sen. Edward D. Baker of Oregon, the president-elect delivered his inaugural address. He was then sworn in by Chief Justice of the United States Roger Brooke Taney, author of the Dred Scott decision.

Directed in large part to the Southern states, seven of which had seceded and established the Confederate States of America, the inaugural address was a closely reasoned plea for the Union. Approaching a conclusion, Lincoln said:

> *You* have no oath registered in Heaven to destroy the government, while *I* shall have the most solemn one to "preserve, protect and defend" it.[1]

As is well known, Lincoln was personally an intensely complicated man. I suggest that as president he was quite uncomplicated. Having taken an oath to preserve, protect, and defend the United States, he proposed to do just that. From the beginning, all men and all measures were determined by a single standard: the capacity to help or hurt the defeat of the rebellion.

Sandburg's Lincoln, the mythic hero, was folksy, sweet, and kind, a wholly sympathetic character. These were surely aspects of the man. But as Stephen B. Oates has recently pointed out, Lincoln was "a tough wartime President, flexing his executive muscles and expanding his war powers whenever necessity demanded."[2] He had taken an oath. He was dead in earnest and resolute.

Article II of the Constitution of the United States is almost quaint in the brevity of its description of the powers of the president. It says that "the Executive power shall be vested in" him. Section 2 states that he "shall be commander-in-chief of the army and navy." But until the Lincoln years, with the possible exception of the tenure of Andrew Jackson, the government of the United States was essentially a congressional government. Confronted with the unprecedented crisis and without significant precedent in terms of the role and power of his office, Lincoln proceeded as commander-in-chief to *create* the modern presidency, an office of great political power.

In the midst of the secession crisis, Lincoln authorized military commanders to declare martial law and thereby sanctioned arbitrary arrest and trial and conviction by military commission instead of the conventional courts. He also authorized the supension of the writ of habeas corpus.[3] It is worthwhile at the outset briefly to discuss the significance of arbitrary arrest, military commission trials, and supension of habeas corpus.

According to the American legal system, one may not be lawfully arrested unless he is suspected of committing a specific act that is proscribed by generally applicable law. The person arrested must be promptly brought before a conventional court and charged with the act. An arbitrary arrest has no such requirements. One may be seized at will and either charged with an offense known or unknown to the generally applicable law or, as was sometimes the case during the Civil War, retained in prison and never charged at all.

Jurisdiction is a lawyer's word, the kind of word that causes lay persons to dislike lawyers. It means *power*. In the law, an authority with jurisdiction over us has the legal power to force our obedience. Thus, the conventional courts may subpoena us, and the police authorities will seize us if we do not comply with the subpoena. The conventional court can sentence us to jail, and the police authorities will take us there and hold us. These conventional jurisdictions are, of course, subject to the Constitution and statutes that restrict and condition their power. They may only act according to due process, according to law. If the government sets up a collateral jurisdiction, that is, an agency with the *power* of the courts but without the constitutional and statutory restrictions and conditions of that power, a profound change in our status has occurred. A military commission is an example of such a collateral jurisdiction.

The writ of habeas corpus is a direction from the conventional court to an agency that is detaining someone. The writ commands the agency to produce the person in court and to justify the detention. If the detention cannot be justified, the prisoner is released by the court. The writ tests the legality of the detention, not the guilt or innocence of the prisoner. Article I of the Constitution, the article concerning the Congress, authorizes the suspension of the writ of habeas corpus "when in cases of rebellion or invasion the public safety may require it." It seems plain that the Lincoln program of arbitrary arrest and military commission jurisdiction was dependent on the unavailability of the writ. If habeas corpus had been available to a prisoner, a court would have released him because of the arbitrary character of the arrest or the unconventional military trial.

This then was the Lincoln administration's program for coping with the problem of dissent. Lincoln was sensitive to the anomaly of his situation. He addressed this issue in his message of July 4, 1861, to the Special Session of the Congress. Referring to the fact that he had authorized the military "to arrest, and detain, without resort to the ordinary processes and forms of law," he acknowledged that "the legality and propriety of what has been done" were questioned, and "the attention of the country has been called to the proposition that one who is sworn to 'take care that the laws be faithfully executed' should not himself violate them." Lincoln then described the crisis of the Union and stated his rationale, essentially that of necessity. Rhetorically, he asked: "Are all the laws, *but one*, to go unexecuted, and the government itself go to pieces, lest that one be violated?"[4]

A more detailed statement of Lincoln's position appears in his remarkable letter of June 12, 1863, to Erastus Corning. In this letter Lincoln responded to resolutions of May 16, 1863, made by New York Democrats meeting in Albany.[5] Referring to Clement L. Vallandingham of Ohio, a prominent Democratic politician and an articulate and intemperate critic of Lincoln and the war effort whose arrest had prompted the Albany resolutions, Lincoln stated his often-quoted epigram: "Must I shoot a simple-minded soldier boy who deserts, while I must not touch a hair of a wiley agitator who induces him to desert?" The popularity of this statement has, it seems to me, distracted us from a more careful consideration of the Corning letter.

Abe Lincoln was not a careless man. He was a highly competent, technical lawyer. As is well known, he also had an uncommon facility with the language. When he set forth his views in a letter that he expected to be made public, I think that we may assume that the letter unambiguously reflected his state of mind. Setting aside its plainly political aspects, I read the Corning letter as Lincoln's brief on the issue of the propriety of his administration's treatment of dissent by means of arbitrary arrest, military trial, and the suspension of the writ of habeas corpus. One should read the letter to grasp it fully, but I will briefly describe it.

At the outset, Lincoln asserted his conclusion that the unusual proceedings that the New York Democrats complained of were *not* unconstitutional. They were, he said, within "the exceptions of the constitution, and . . . indispensable to the public safety." He then presented his arguments to support this conclusion.

Beginning as a good lawyer should with a statement of the facts, Lincoln contended that, at the time that he took office, persons sympathetic to secession had "pervaded all departments of the government, and nearly all communities of the people," and that the South relied on this fact and the ability of these sympathizers to subvert the government under the "cover" [Lincoln's word] of free speech, free press, and habeas corpus. Continuing with his factual premises, Lincoln then discussed the conventional civil courts. They were, he said, organized to try individuals or small groups of people, in quiet times, on "charges of crimes well defined in the law"; they were not competent to deal with massive groups of disloyal people in the loyal states whose acts damaged the war effort but did not constitute a "defined crime."

Lincoln then turned to the law. Referring to Section 9 of Article I of the Constitution, that is, the provision permitting the suspension of habeas corpus "when in cases of Rebellion or Invasion, the public Safety may require it," he contended that this language authorized not only the suspension of the writ but also arbitrary arrest, military commission trial, and the remaining aspects of his program. Specifically, he relied on this language of the Constitution in regard to the arrest and holding of persons "who can not be proved to be guilty of defined crime." Such arrests, he conceded, were not for what had been done by a defendant, but "for what probably would be done." Thus, in Lincoln's words, such arrests were "preventive," so as "to silence the agitator." With reference to Vallandingham, Lincoln stated his understanding that Vallandingham had been speaking to prevent the raising of troops. This, he said, was "warring upon the military; and this gave the military constitutional jurisdiction to lay hands on him."

The president concluded with a reassurance. He expressed confidence that the "right of public discussion, the liberty of speech and the press, the law of evidence, trial by jury, and Habeas corpus" would return once the rebellion was defeated.

Three aspects of the president's analysis seem to me to be noteworthy. In the first place, there is the letter's candid acknowledgement that arbitrary arrest, the military commissions, and suspension of habeas corpus imposed on the traditional American constitutional framework in fundamental ways. Preventive detention, instead of arrest for the commission of a generally prohibited act, freedom of speech, freedom of the press, trial by jury, and the law of evidence were also at stake. In addition, Lincoln's analysis of the Vallandingham arrest suggests that the military establishment had some independent status and autonomy, so that it was free to make and enforce its own laws in reference to people who interfered with it. Finally, there was Lincoln's confidence that the traditional rights would return when the war was over. Surely he hoped that this would happen, but history did not and does not support his optimism.

The Vallandingham Decision

It was the Vallandingham arrest that led to the United States Supreme Court's first opportunity to consider Lincoln's thesis. On April 13, 1863, Maj. Gen. Ambrose Burnside, commanding the Military Department of Ohio, issued General Order No. 38, declaring that thereafter all persons found within his lines "who shall commit acts for the benefit of the enemies of the country, shall be tried as spies or traitors, and if convicted shall suffer death."[6] Among the acts prohibited was declaring sympathy for the enemy. Significantly, the order also referred to punishing violators by sending them into the lines of the enemy. A few days after this order, Burnside issued Special Order No. 135, establishing a military commission to meet in Cincinnati for the trial of persons who might be brought before it. A detail of officers and a judge-advocate were appointed.

On May 1, 1863, at Mount Vernon, Ohio, Vallandingham addressed a political meeting at which he denounced the war as not for the purpose of restoring the Union, but for purposes of establishing a despotism that would free the blacks and enslave the whites. At length and bitterly, the speech attacked Lincoln and the military, including specifically General Burnside's General Order No. 38. On May 5 Vallandingham was arrested at his home by a military detail and taken to Cincinnati and imprisoned. On the following day he was arraigned before the military commission "on a charge of having expressed sympathies for those in arms against the Government . . . and for having uttered in a speech in a public meeting, disloyal sentiments and opinions, with the object and purpose of weakening the power of the government in its efforts for the suppression of an unlawful rebellion."[7]

The defendant challenged the jurisdiction of the military commission and refused to plead. A plea of not guilty was entered by the judge-advocate in his behalf. He was permitted to have counsel and to cross-examine witnesses and call witnesses in his behalf. After an exchange of statements between Vallandingham and the judge-advocate concerning the propriety and constitutionality of the proceeding, the military commission found the defendant guilty, except with reference to one portion of the speech attributed to him, and sentenced him to prison for the duration of the war. The finding and sentence were approved by General Burnside. On May 19, 1863, in commutation of the sentence, President Lincoln ordered that Vallandingham be delivered to a place outside the federal military lines.[8]

Vallandingham's lawyers then petitioned the Supreme Court of the United States for a writ of certiorari, that is, they requested the court to require the judge-advocate general of the army to send the proceedings of the military commission to the court for its review. They contended that the military commission had no jurisdiction to try the defendant. More specifically, Vallandingham argued that he was a civilian and was entitled to trial by jury pursuant to the third section of Article III of the Constitution. He also contended that the offense charged against him was not defined as a crime by the laws of the United States.

As a result of the Congress having "packed" the court in 1863, the Supreme Court to which Vallandingham applied was composed of ten justices. Taney was still the chief justice. Four of the justices were Lincoln appointees: Noah H. Swayne, Samuel F. Miller, David Davis, and Stephen J. Field. Neither Taney nor Justice Miller participated in the Vallandingham deliberations.[9]

Issued February 15, 1864, the opinion in *Ex parte Vallandingham* was written by Justice James M. Wayne, a Georgia Jacksonian. Appointed to the court by Jackson, Wayne had long been an outspoken adherent of the idea of the Federal Union. He wrote for six of the participating justices. Justice Samuel Nelson, a Tyler appointee from New York, concurred in the result but filed no separate opinion.[10]

Wayne's opinion focused on the issue of the Supreme Court's jurisdiction to review the actions of a military commission. It found that its appellate jurisdiction had its source in Article III of the Constitution, pursuant to "such regulations as the Congress shall make." Referring to the acts of Congress, the Court declared that such legislation provided for its jurisdiction to review the rulings of inferior federal courts, but did not extend that jurisdiction to review the decisions of military commissions. It thus denied Vallandingham's petition without an examination of the merits of his claims. Although perhaps defensible on narrow technical grounds, the decision effectively closed the conventional courts to the victims of the administration's program. Had the case been pursued in a different legal form, or had the aged Taney been on hand, it is surely possible that the Court would have had to extend itself further in order to reach its result. The *Detroit Free Press* stated one public reaction: "The Supreme Court has no jurisdiction in matters of individual liberty, unless the party claiming redress can prove he was ravaged according to the law."[11]

Ex parte Milligan

We may now turn to the Milligan prosecution, but that case must be examined within its peculiar context. Indiana Civil War politics have been the subject of three exceptional studies by three able professional historians: Kenneth M. Stampp, Emma Lou Thornbrough, and Gilbert R. Tredway.[12] I must briefly state the facts that their books examine in detail. I concede that I do so with a broad brush.

Oliver P. Morton succeeded to the governorship in January of 1861 on Henry S. Lane's election to the United States Senate by the legislature at its regular session. That session and a special session convened by Morton in April were controlled by the victorious Republicans. The politicians of both parties promptly signaled that the war was not to mute the vigor of their disagreements. My own analysis suggests that there were three common denominators to the political conflict. The issues concerned *principle*, *personalities*, and *patronage*.

The issue of principle involved opinions as to the purpose of the war: was it to maintain the Union, or did it also involve the institution of slavery? A majority of the Democrats rejected the idea of a war against slavery. Perhaps a majority of the Republicans, a new party with many factions, agreed. Morton himself was initially conservative on this question. But there was a significant vocal minority of Republicans, of whom Congressman George W. Julian of the Fifth District was the most prominent, who insisted from the outset that there could be no permanent peace without abolition.[13] This, then, was the first issue, the relationship between slavery and the war, and for a long time the politicians maneuvered around it like medieval churchmen.

In terms of personalities, there were, of course, many, but Morton was *the* personality. According to Kenneth M. Stampp, and any reading of the press or the legislative history of the period surely supports him, "Governor Morton . . . was . . . frequently the central figure in these renewed political conflicts." Stampp asserts that "to a considerable extent this was caused by the Governor's own personality and ambition. Morton was an exceptionally able executive, but he was blunt, pugnacious, ruthless, and completely lacking in a sense of humor." Wholly intolerant of disagreement, his approach toward those who opposed him, in and out of his party, was to harass them and impugn their motives and their character. Both the Democrats and such Republican leaders as Julian and the president of the

Indiana senate and speaker of the Indiana house were heavily at odds with Morton.[14]

And then there was patronage, in those days crude and unpretentious. Politicians and their followers were always sensitive to it and willing to fight about it. The very fact of the war significantly enlarged the scope of patronage, and the conflict about it increased in proportion. Not the least of the new subjects of patronage was power to appoint regimental and company officers for Indiana regiments. During the war, 18,884 such commissions were issued to Hoosiers.[15] The governor's control of this power was the subject of much political and legislative activity.

The factional and partisan bickering reached its first crescendo as the 1862 elections approached. It is only fair to the antagonists to acknowledge that additional issues of principle had emerged and were very real. Arbitrary arrest, suspension of the writ of habeas corpus, emancipation, the power of the presidency, tariff increases, the additional calls for volunteers, and the proposal of a military draft were easy to get excited about. And the war was killing a lot of Indiana soldiers and was going badly. The summer of 1862 saw McClellan's withdrawal from the Peninsula, the defeat at Second Bull Run, the invasion of Kentucky, and Lee's movement into Maryland. Kenneth Stampp fairly describes the Republican response to the Democrats' political exploitation of the state of the war. It was, he writes, "fierce and partisan . . . raising the cry of treason and identifying any sort of criticism with that term. Only traitors, they inferred, would denounce President Lincoln or Governor Morton while rebels were trying to destroy the nation."[16] George W. Julian was later to admit that "loyalty to Republicanism was . . . accepted as the best evidence of loyalty to the country."[17]

In his keynote speech to the 1862 Republican state convention, Morton spoke darkly of the Northwest Conspiracy, which he described as a Democratic scheme to take Kentucky and the states of the Old Northwest out of the Union and to ally them with the South. He told of secret treasonable societies in Indiana and warned that they would be suppressed.[18] In August, with Morton's involvement, a federal grand jury in Indianapolis issued an exposé of the Knights of the Golden Circle, allegedly a secret Democratic treasonable society. The report was widely used by the Republicans in the 1862 canvass.[19]

On October 14, 1862, the Democrats carried the state by 9,000 votes. The governorship was not at issue, but the Democrats took control of the rest of the statehouse and both houses of the General Assembly. Having studied the campaign and the activities of the Democrats in detail, Stampp concludes that "the Indiana Democracy of 1862 was eminently loyal. While it criticized methods, it campaigned as a war party and demanded suppression of the rebellion by force of arms."[20] Frank L. Klement of Marquette University, also a keen student of dissent during the war, agrees with Stampp, but he accurately observes that the Indiana Democrats "played partisan politics viciously while the nation's life was at stake."[21]

Having approached the brink of political destructiveness during the 1862 campaign, the parties proceeded in the 1863 legislature to go over the brink. Never one to assume a defensive posture, Morton fired the first shots. On January 3, as the legislators arrived in Indianapolis, the governor wired Secretary Stanton that he had been "advised that it is the intent of the Legislature . . . to pass a joint resolution to acknowledge the Southern Confederacy and urge the Northwest to dissolve all constitutional relations with the New England States."[22] Although there were many issues and side shows, three Democratic legislative plans, all blatantly political, seem to have created the ultimate impasse: reapportionment of the legislature and congressional districts; the establishment of an executive council, composed of the Democratic secretary of state, auditor, treasurer, and attorney general, to whom the governor was to be required to defer; and a military bill drafted so as to limit the governor's power over the large state military establishment. Alleging that these were treasonable proposals, on February 26, 1863, all but four Republicans in the House of Representatives withdrew and traveled to Madison so as to cross the river if the sergeant-at-arms came to bring them back. The legislature was deprived of a constitutional quorum and came to a standstill. Since no appropriation bills had been passed, each party assumed that the other would make the political concessions necessary to reconstitute the legislature, but these concessions were not made. The legislature adjourned without appropriating funds to conduct the state for the ensuing two years.[23]

The redoubtable Morton proceeded to conduct the state government by other means: War Department funding, loans from various counties on the basis of the governor's personal receipts, and loans from a New York banking firm. The state financial officers, the treasurer and auditor, were ignored. The funds were kept in a guarded safe in the governor's office under the administration of a Morton creation, the Bureau of Finance, headed by his military secretary, William Henry Harrison Terrell.[24]

The bitterness and partisanship that marked the 1862 election and the 1863 legislative breakdown continued unabated into 1864, as did the war itself. The 1864 state election in Indiana was scheduled for October 11, to be followed by the federal election on November 8. This time Governor Morton himself was running for reelection as the nominee of the Republicans, for the time being identified as the Union party. The war was two years older. All of the real issues of 1862 were there. More lives had been lost, and the final, bloody Virginia Campaign had begun in May. The loyalty issue was as vigorous as ever. Morton and his allies approached the campaign with the renewed claim that the Democrats supported the South and were in fact treasonable.[25]

Gen. Alvin P. Hovey, a native Hoosier and former colonel of the Twenty-fourth Indiana Volunteers, had been a prewar Democrat. A combat veteran, in 1864 he was the Commander of the Military District of Indiana. He shared Governor Morton's view that Morton's political foes were disloyal.[26] In the midst of the heated political campaign, with Morton's complicity, Hovey on September 17, 1864, issued Special Orders No. 129 authorizing a military commission "to meet at the United States Court Rooms in the City of Indianapolis on the nineteenth day of September, 1864, . . . for the trial of . . . such . . . prisoners as may be brought before it."[27] General Hovey had already undertaken within the period prior to the elections a series of military arrests which involved numerous Indiana citizens, including eight men prominently connected with the Democratic party: William M. Harrison, secretary of the Democratic Club of Marion County; Harrison H. Dodd; William A. Bowles, a delegate to the 1864 Indiana Democratic Convention; Joseph J. Bingham, editor of the *Indianapolis Daily State Sentinel* and chairman of the Democratic State Central Committee; Horace Heffren, editor of the *Washington Democrat* of Salem, Indiana, formerly a state legislator and officer in Indiana volunteer regiments; Stephen Horsey; Andrew Humphreys, a leading Democrat from the Greene and Sullivan County area; and

Lambdin P. Milligan, a Huntington lawyer. Milligan, who gave his name to the later decision of the Supreme Court of the United States, was a harsh and angry critic of Lincoln and Morton. He hated the fact of the war, concentrating his fire on the threat to constitutional government that he believed the war represented. Not a mainstream Democrat, he had unsuccessfully sought the Democratic gubernatorial nomination in 1864. Two more Democratic leaders, David T. Yeakel and James B. Wilson, were arrested after the state election but before the national election.[28]

The arrests and the later trials were preceded and accompanied by vigorous and partisan publicity. This aspect of the matter originated with an exposé of a secret society, the Sons of Liberty, published in the *Indianapolis Daily Journal* on June 29, 1864, and continued with unusual intensity in the same organ after its acquisition on August 28, 1864, by William R. Holloway, Governor Morton's brother-in-law and private secretary.[29] The War Department in Washington cooperated. On October 8, 1864, Judge Advocate General Holt issued a lengthy report on the Order of the American Knights, "alias The Sons of Liberty." The report identified several of the defendants, including Dodd and Milligan, as officers of the society in Indiana and alleged that it was planning an armed insurrection and had 75,000 to 125,000 members in the state. A Northwestern Confederacy, in alliance with the South, was identified by Holt as a goal of the Sons of Liberty.[30]

General Hovey's military commission was initially composed of seven Indiana military officers. Maj. Henry L. Burnett of Ohio was the judge-advocate. It is the opinion of professional historians who have studied the events that several members of the commission were biased and partisan and had accepted Governor Morton's premise that disagreement and dissent were tantamount to disloyalty and treason.[31] Col. Benjamin Spooner had declared publicly that all persons not voting the straight Republican ticket were "traitors."[32] Four of the commissioners, including Spooner, delivered rousing speeches to Republican rallies while the trials were in progress.[33]

The first of the defendants to be tried was Harrison H. Dodd. The specifications involving Dodd alleged that he did "conspire against the Government . . . joining and organizing a subversive society for that purpose." He was also charged with a plan "to seize by force the United States arsenals . . . to release rebel prisoners at Camp

Douglas, Camp Morton, Camp Chase, and Johnson's Island, to arm said prisoners, and then march into Kentucky to cooperate with the rebels." Finally, it was alleged that Dodd had aroused "hostility to the Government" through public addresses and secretly arming subversive society members "for the purpose of resisting the laws of the United States."[34] Like the later trial of Milligan, this one featured the Sons of Liberty and the Northwest Conspiracy. The principal witness was a government private detective, Felix G. Stidger, who had infiltrated Dodd's group, befriended Dodd, and now testified at length concerning the alleged plots. Before the trial was completed, Dodd escaped from imprisonment and fled to Canada. On October 10, 1864, the military commission found Dodd guilty of each charge and specification and sentenced him to be hanged, which decision was approved by the War Department.[35]

On the day following Dodd's conviction *in absentia*, the Republicans swept the Indiana state elections with substantial majorities.[36] But the national election was still to come, and Milligan and the other prominent prisoners were still to be dealt with. In the skirmishing on the eve of the trial, the charges against Joseph J. Bingham, William M. Harrison, David T. Yeakel, and James B. Wilson were dismissed. Horace Heffren was released after the trial began. He and Harrison and Wilson were to appear as prosecution witnesses, presumably in consideration of the dismissal. This left Milligan, Horsey, Bowles, and Humphreys. On October 21, with the national elections looming, the military commission convened. To the original detail of the seven officers five additional colonels had been added to the commission.[37] There were five charges:

1. Conspiracy against the government of the United States;
2. Affording aid and comfort to the rebels against the authority of the United States;
3. Inciting insurrection;
4. Disloyal practices; and
5. Violations of the laws of war.[38]

It was more specifically alleged that the defendants had established a secret military organization and planned to seize arsenals, release Confederate prisoners, raise an armed force, join with the Confederate forces to invade Indiana, Illinois, and Kentucky, and make war on the United States. Because of the prosecution's conspiracy theory, the acts of any one of the defendants could be imputed to them all. And because the already convicted escapee Dodd was a member of the conspiracy, his acts were included in the imputation.[39]

Each of the defendants was represented by counsel. Milligan's lawyer was John R. Coffroth, a Huntington Democrat, who braved the hostility of the judge-advocate and some of the members of the commission, as well as the prosecution's occasional efforts to implicate him in the alleged conspiracy.[40] Coffroth and the other defendants' counsel unsuccessfully raised the issue of the military commission's jurisdiction, and the trial ensued. Because this paper is concerned with the *legal* issue of jurisdiction, the evidence is beyond its scope, but some flavor of the proceeding may be gathered from this colloquy in which the judge-advocate questioned the newly cooperative Horace Heffren about the allegedly treasonable Sons of Liberty:

> Q. Of what political faith were the majority of the men comprising the organization?
> A. They were all Democrats.
> Q. State whether any other class of men were admitted, or was it a *sine qua non* that a man must be a Democrat?
> A. I do not think anyone would have got in unless he professed to be a Democrat.[41]

The Republicans carried Indiana in the national elections on November 8, and the military commission on December 10, 1864, reached its decision. Milligan, Bowles, and Horsey were found guilty and sentenced to be hanged. Humphreys was also convicted and sentenced to imprisonment at hard labor for the duration of the war. With President Lincoln's approval, General Hovey promptly modified Humphreys's sentence. Humphreys was released providing he did not take part in any acts opposing the war and did not leave two specified townships in Greene County.[42]

One of the several curiosities of the Milligan case is the effort made to obtain clemency for the three men who were to be hanged. This is a story in itself, but this paper must briefly allude to it. Col. William E. McLean, one of the commissioners, wrote to Lincoln in behalf of Milligan. Disclosing that he had dissented from the commission's findings, McLean stated that "the evidence adduced wholly failed to sustain the charge of conspiracy" against Milligan. According to the colonel's letter, Milligan's outright release was called for by "common justice and the popular sentiment of the people of Indiana."[43] Joseph E. McDonald, the Indiana Democratic nominee for governor in 1864 and a political foe of Milligan, now acting with Coffroth as counsel for Milligan, urged Lincoln to pardon all three of the men.[44] But most surprising were Morton's efforts in behalf of the defendants.

With Lincoln's death, the issue of clemency passed to Andrew Johnson. On May 16, 1865, three days before the execution date, Johnson commuted Horsey's sentence to life imprisonment and postponed the execution of Milligan and Bowles to June 2.[45] On May 24, 1865, Morton dispatched former Congressman John U. Pettit to see the president with directions "most earnestly to plead for the commutation of their punishment to life imprisonment."[46] On May 30, 1865, the president acted to commute the sentences to life imprisonment.[47]

In the midst of the clemency activity, on May 10, 1865, Milligan's lawyers filed a petition for writ of habeas corpus in the circuit court of the United States for the district of Indiana, sitting in Indianapolis.[48] Similar proceedings were instituted in behalf of Horsey and Bowles. Pursuant to the procedure, the application was considered by two judges, Justice David Davis of the United States Supreme Court, who was also a judge of the federal circuit that included Indiana, and Judge Thomas Drummond, a circuit judge. The procedure further provided that if these two judges disagreed, the questions at issue were to be certified to the Supreme Court of the United States.

Milligan's petition was based on an act of Congress that was intended to moot the question of whether the president or the Congress had the constitutional right to suspend the writ of habeas corpus as authorized by Section 9 of Article I of the Constitution. This issue had been active throughout the war. The legislation also responded to other aspects of the Lincoln administration's program to cope with dissent. Effective on March 3, 1863, it was identified as "An Act Relating to Habeas Corpus and Regulating Judicial Proceedings in Certain Cases."[49] It authorized the president to suspend the writ of habeas corpus when in his judgment the public safety required it. Referring to the statute, Lincoln had issued a proclamation accordingly on September 15, 1863. The statute further directed the secretaries of state and war to furnish to the federal judges in states where the courts were operating the names of all persons held there in custody. It also stipulated that if a grand jury met after the list was furnished and did not indict the prisoner, he was entitled to be discharged. Finally, to avoid frustration of the statute by the failure of the cabinet officers to submit the list, the act provided that if the list was not furnished and twenty days had elapsed from the time of the arrest and termination of the session of the grand jury, the prisoner was entitled to a discharge. Milligan alleged, and it was a fact, that a federal grand jury had met in Indianapolis during January of 1865 and had not indicted him.

It may be noted that Vallandingham did not pursue this procedure or rely on this statute. It seems likely that a federal grand jury had met in his district, and it is known that he was not indicted. But he proceeded in 1863 by the certiorari route. I do not suggest that the decision in the case would have been any different had Vallandingham invoked the Milligan procedure—the war was in full cry at the time that the Supreme Court considered the Vallandingham case—but the speculation is an interesting one.

In the circuit court sitting in Indianapolis, Justice Davis and Judge Drummond were unable to agree on the issues presented by Milligan's petition. Accordingly, three issues were certified to the Supreme Court:

>   1st.   On the facts stated in said petition and exhibits, ought a writ of habeas corpus to be issued?
>   2nd.   On the facts stated in said petition and exhibits, ought the said Lambdin P. Milligan to be discharged from custody as in said petition prayed?
>   3rd.   Whether, upon the facts stated in said petition and exhibits, the Military Commission mentioned therein had jurisdiction legally to try and sentence said Milligan in manner and form as in said petition and exhibits is stated.[50]

It should be understood that the Supreme Court was not considering the charges against Milligan; it did not evaluate or consider the evidence adduced before the military commission. It was concerned entirely with questions of law. In short, regardless of the charges and evidence, the issues were whether the military commission proceedings were constitutional and whether Milligan was entitled to be discharged.

The case was argued on March 5 and 13, 1866, approximately a year after Appomattox and Lincoln's death. The Court was the same one that had heard Vallandingham's petition for certiorari except that Salmon P. Chase, appointed by Lincoln in December of 1864, had replaced Taney as the Chief Justice.[51]

Distinguished lawyers represented the parties. In addition to Coffroth and J. E. McDonald, Milligan's lawyers were A. L. Roache, David Dudley Field, James A. Garfield, and Jeremiah S. Black. Field, who was the brother of Justice Stephen Field of the Supreme Court, was a well-known New Yorker associated with efforts to reform the legal system of that state. Garfield, of course, was a member of Congress from Ohio and a future president. Black, who practiced frequently before the Supreme Court, had been Buchanan's attorney general and secretary of state. Although fewer in number, the United States surely had adequate counsel in Attorney General James Speed, Henry Stanbery, and the colorful and controversial Benjamin F. Butler. Butler had been a prewar Massachusetts politician, a political major general during the war, and was later to be a congressman and governor of Massachusetts.[52]

On April 3, 1866, the chief justice announced the order of the Court: a writ of habeas corpus was to be issued; Milligan was entitled to be discharged, a decision expressly based on the March 3, 1863, act of Congress; and the military commission had no jurisdiction to try and sentence Milligan. The same order was entered in the Bowles and Horsey companion cases. The chief justice announced that the opinion of the Court and any dissents would be read at the next term of the Court.

On December 17, 1866, Justice David Davis delivered the majority opinion, writing for himself and five of the other members of the Court. The opinion at first disposed of two procedural issues raised by the government.[53] Then it turned to the merits. Noting that Milligan was a civilian and a resident of a state in which the civil courts were functioning, Davis stated that "it is the birthright of every American citizen when charged with [a] crime to be tried and punished according to law." Davis then identified the constitutional provisions affecting the administration of criminal justice: trial by jury (Article III, Section 2); security against unreasonable search and seizure and the requirement of a judicial warrant, based on probable cause, before arrest (Fourth Amendment); grand jury indictment and due process (Fifth Amendment); and speedy and public trial by jury (Sixth Amendment). These, according to the opinion, had not been available to Milligan. The opinion then states:

> Every trial involves the exercise of judicial power; and from what source did the Military Commission . . . derive their authority? Certainly no part of the judicial power of the country was conferred on them; because the Constitution expressly vests it 'in one Supreme Court and such inferior courts as the Congress may from time to time ordain and establish'. . . .

The government had presented numerous grounds for the propriety of the military commission. The manner in which the opinion met several of them concerns the significance of the case.

Responding to a contention that the laws and usages of war supported the jurisdiction of the military commander, Justice Davis wrote: "Congress could grant no such power; and to the honor of our national legislature be it said, it has never been provoked . . . even to attempt its exercise." To the argument that martial law gave a military commander the power to suspend civilian rights and subject civilians and soldiers to his will, Davis responded: " . . . if true, republican government is a failure, and there is an end of liberty regulated by law." In any event, according to the opinion, "Martial rule can never exist where the courts are open. . . . " Thus, martial law would be confined to "the theatre of actual military operations, where war really prevails" and "there is a necessity to furnish a substitute for the civil authority, thus overthrown. . . . " As if responding to Lincoln's contention in his letter to Corning about exceptions to the Constitution during the Civil War, Davis adverted to the risk of evil or unwise leaders, unlike Lincoln, and wrote: "No doctrine, involving more pernicious consequences, was ever invented by the wit of man than that any of its provisions can be suspended during any of the great exigencies of government." Finally, it will be recalled that Lincoln had relied on the language of the Constitution's authorization of the suspension of the writ of habeas corpus "when in cases of rebellion . . . the public safety may require it" to justify suspension of the writ as well as his other acts: arbitrary arrest, military commission jurisdiction, and limitations on freedom of speech, assembly, and press. Davis rejected this rationale. Referring generally to the Constitution's restrictions on governmental power, Davis said: "Not one of these safeguards can the President or Congress or the Judiciary disturb, except the one concerning the writ of habeas corpus."

The chief justice and justices Miller, Swayne, and Wayne filed a separate opinion authored by the chief justice. It is a somewhat curious document. It agrees with the majority on each of the three certified questions but disagrees with several of the dicta of the majority. Thus, Chase wrote that although the Congress had not authorized the military commission that tried Milligan, the minority believed that Congress had the power to do so. Regarding the writ of habeas corpus, Chase stated that when the writ is suspended, the Executive is authorized to arrest as well as detain and that "there are cases in which, the privilege of the writ being suspended, trial and punishment by military commission, in states where the civil courts are open, may be authorized by Congress, as well as arrest and detention." It appears therefore that the minority might have accepted the Lincoln program regarding dissent, although not necessarily in Milligan's case, had it been enacted by the Congress. The minority concluded with this reassurance: "We have no apprehension that this power, under our American system of government, in which all official authority is derived from the people, and exercised under direct responsibility to the people, is more likely to be abused than the power to regulate commerce or the power to borrow money."

Lambdin P. Milligan returned to Huntington and his law practice. In 1868 he filed suit for false arrest and false imprisonment in the Huntington Circuit Court against Morton, General Hovey, several members of the military commission, certain witnesses before the commission, and others whom Milligan believed were implicated. The case was removed to the Federal Circuit Court in Indianapolis and, after much delay, came to a jury trial in 1871. Again a distinguished battery of lawyers was involved. Milligan's counsel included Thomas A. Hendricks, former United States Senator from Indiana, later to be Tilden's running mate in 1876 and Grover Cleveland's vice-president.[54] Benjamin Harrison was chief counsel for the defendants. Although Milligan sought thousands of dollars in damages, state and federal indemnity statutes limited his claim to $5.00, plus the costs of the litigation.

It must again be emphasized that Milligan's guilt or innocence of the allegations before the 1864 military commission were not directly at issue. The issue in a legal sense was whether he had been arrested and held unlawfully in view of the Supreme Court decision. It nevertheless appears that many of the 1864 witnesses appeared and that the trial was rife with the political overtones of the military commission proceeding. At length the jury found for Milligan and awarded him the permissible $5.00 and costs estimated at $1,200.[55] It was the view of Governor Morton's allies that the small damage award somehow vindicated Morton and the military commission proceedings. In view of the statutory limitation on damages this seems to me an unwarranted conclusion.

Commentary

So much for *Ex parte Milligan* as a legal proposition. What of the facts? Was Milligan guilty of the charges against him?

The circumstances of Milligan's trial before the military commission suggest to me that although he was a bitter and sometimes irresponsible critic of Lincoln, Morton, and the Republican party, the judge-advocate did not prove him guilty of the offenses with which he was charged. That, of course, was the prosecution's burden. Kenneth M. Stampp, Gilbert R. Tredway, and Frank L. Klement, all of whom have studied the proceedings from the standpoint of guilt or innocence, are unconvinced of his guilt.[56] As a lawyer, I believe that a trial prompted by political motives, before politically biased military officers, without the rules of evidence, with questionable informers as witnesses, and surrounded by lurid publicity is, in effect, a nullity. What is customarily identified as due process involves not simply a question of fairness to the accused. It is the only kind of forum in which there is a practical chance of establishing the truth.

There are, of course, other questions. Were there Indiana secret societies acting in behalf of secession? Was there a Northwest Conspiracy? There were indeed several secret societies, including the Knights of the Golden Circle, the Order of American Knights, and the Sons of Liberty. They were composed of dissenters, typically embittered Democrats who were out of the mainstream of their party. Some of them, including H. H. Dodd, were in contact with Confederate agents and discussed the release of Confederate prisoners and acts of war. Recent scholarship suggests that the membership of the secret societies was extremely small and that they did not have the will, the influence, or the means of interfering with the prosecution of the war. The Northwest Conspiracy also existed in the minds of Confederate agents and a small group of midwestern and Kentucky dissenters, again probably including H. H. Dodd, but it, too, was never a significant threat. Both the size and influence of the secret societies and the significance of the Northwest Conspiracy were inflated by Morton and the Republicans for partisan and personal political purposes.[57]

And there is, at last, the ultimate question. There is, conceptually, a difference between, on the one hand, disagreement about the war or with the Lincoln administration's means of prosecuting the war and support of the Southern bid for independence on the other. The latter, it would seem, is appropriately called "disloyalty." The ultimate question, therefore, is whether or not there was significant or widespread disloyalty in Indiana. Were Hoosiers, in the main, for the Union, or were they willing to see it sundered?

In 1869 the state published the eight-volume *Report of the Adjutant General of the State of Indiana*. The adjutant general was W. H. H. Terrell, Morton's friend and appointee. In volume I the report describes "Internal State Troubles," concerning the entire course of Indiana politics during the war, including the conspiracies, secret societies, and military commission trials. It is, of course, the Morton view of these events.

At the outset, Terrell states his premises. The rebel states "relied upon a greater power than their own in their attempt to displace the old Government by a new confederacy. . . . That power was the spirit of dissension, of faction, of treason in the North." This "disloyal feeling" "was extensive enough, and malignant enough" to accomplish the success of the rebellion. The report then states that this feeling was "strong enough to take Indiana out of loyal hands in 1862, and leave her nothing but the iron will and unfailing sagacity of her Governor to prevent her own soil being made the scene of endless and ruinous local wars." Terrell ultimately contends that it was the South's knowledge of the extent of treason and disloyalty in the North that caused the South to begin the war.[58]

These extravagant claims plainly suggest that Indiana was disloyal, that it teetered on the brink of secession, and that it was held to the Union cause by Governor Morton. These beliefs have long been part of the folk tradition of Indiana. Indeed, it was taught as history in Indiana schools in the 1930s and 1940s when some of us were in school. It lingers among us today. It is, of course, an extension of the politics of the war. It may incidentally be noted that the postwar politics of the Gilded Age, the days of "the Bloody Shirt," essentially embraced this proposition.

Certain statistics seem to me to answer the Morton tradition. At the same time, these statistics support the conclusion that the secret societies and conspiracies were not significant in numbers or influence.

The Indiana election returns of 1860 gave the four candidates the following totals:

> Lincoln, the Republican—139,000
> Douglas, the Democrat—116,000
> Bell, Constitutional Union—5,000
> Breckinridge, Southern Democrat—12,000[59]

Breckinridge was the outright Southern candidate. Notwithstanding the usual fog of politics, it is plain that all of the others were firmly Union candidates. Thus less than 5 percent of the 1860 Indiana voters supported the Southern position.

Of more significance are the data assembled by William F. Fox in his work *Regimental Losses in the American Civil War*. According to Fox, 74.3 percent of Indiana's military population was enrolled in the federal armies, second only to Delaware, which furnished 74.8 percent. According to Fox, "it appears that the States of Delaware and Indiana were preeminently loyal, contributing more largely in proportion to their military population than any of their sister states."[60] According to Terrell, these soldiers were overwhelmingly volunteers.[61]

Finally, Gilbert R. Tredway has made an analysis of Indiana's volunteers by congressional district. The three banner Democratic districts were the first, second, and seventh. All three went Democratic in 1860, 1862, and 1864. Their Republican counterparts, the "safe" Republican districts, were the fifth, sixth, eighth, and ninth. Military quotas were established by congressional district according to population. Men were drafted in a district only to the extent that sufficient men did not volunteer to meet the district's quota. The Democratic districts consistently furnished more volunteers in proportion to their population than did the Republican districts until the last call of the war in December of 1864. Only then did the

Republican districts surpass the Democratic districts in volunteers. This was true in spite of the fact that the Democratic districts consistently paid smaller bounties to stimulate volunteers.[62]

In the majority opinion in *Ex parte Milligan*, Justice Davis, perhaps generally aware of these facts, discussed the status of the federal court in Indianapolis. "It needed no bayonets to protect it, and required no military aide to execute its judgements. It was held in a state, eminently distinguished for patriotism. . . ."[63]

Conclusion

The Lincoln administration's program to cope with dissent and those who disagreed with the administration presented a classic confrontation between government power and personal liberty, as that liberty is defined in the American political and legal process. It was a confrontation occurring in an authentic crisis. *Ex parte Milligan* stands on the side of personal liberty. The decision is a rebuke to those who would forego liberty in the interest of security.

It occurs to me that many of us today do not really comprehend what the personal liberty provisions of the Constitution are all about. In a given conflict between the popular will and the Constitution, many of us seem to miss the constitutional point and react instead on the basis of our response to the merits of the proposal of the popular will. But the point is that the Constitution is essentially a statement of limitations on the popular will and on the government as the agent of the popular will. The heart of any civil liberties case, therefore, concerns not whether the people approve of the act of government but a more fundamental question: should the government have this power? Inevitably, this question requires a consideration of whether or not the power at issue is subject to abuse. In an obscenity case, for example, the issue is not how one feels about allegedly obscene materials. The issue is whether government should have the power to limit what we read, in the light of the fact that governments have historically abused the power to censor.

In *Ex parte Milligan*, the Supreme Court was unwilling to accord the Lincoln administration the power of military commission jurisdiction. An express reason for this denial of power was the risk of abuse by other presidents or in other circumstances. It seems clear to me that the Supreme Court was correct.

Notes

1. Roy P. Basler, ed., *The Collected Works of Abraham Lincoln* 8 vols. (New Brunswick, N.J.: Rutgers University Press, 1953), 4:271. This source is hereinafter cited as *Collected Works*.

2. Stephen B. Oates, *Abraham Lincoln, the Man Behind the Myths* (New York: Harper & Row Publishers, 1984), 120.

3. See, for example, Lincoln to Gen. Winfield Scott, April 25 and 27, 1861, in *Collected Works*, 4:344, 347, and Lincoln's proclamation of May 10, 1861, concerning the state of Florida in ibid., 4:364–65. See also Lincoln's proclamation of September 24, 1862, suspending the writ, establishing martial law, and authorizing trial and punishment by military commission with respect to "all Rebels and Insurgents, their aiders and abettors within the United States, and all persons discouraging volunteer enlistments, resisting military drafts, or guilty of any disloyal practice, affording aid and comfort to the Rebels. . . . " Ibid., 5: 436–37. See also William W. Winthrop, *Military Law and Precedents* (Washington, D.C.: Government Printing Office, 1920), 833–34.

4. *Collected Works*, 4:429–30.

5. All quotations from Corning letter are in ibid., 6:260–69.

6. *Ex parte In the Matter of Clement L. Vallandingham, Petitioner*, February 15, 1864, 68 U.S. (1 Wall.) 243, 17 L. Ed. 589. The facts of the Vallandingham case are taken from the Supreme Court report. The case is described and discussed by numerous authorities, including Frank L. Klement, *Dark Lanterns—Secret Political Societies, Conspiracies, and Treason Trials in the Civil War* (Baton Rouge and London: Louisiana State University Press, 1984); J. G. Randall, *Lincoln, the President* (New York: Dodd, Mead & Co., 1952), vol. 3; and Frank L. Klement, *The Limits of Dissent: Clement L. Vallandingham & the Civil War* (Lexington: University of Kentucky Press, 1970).

7. *Ex parte Vallandingham*, 17 L. Ed. 589, 590.

8. As is well known, Vallandingham was delivered to the Confederate lines in Tennessee. He went to Richmond, ran the blockade, and moved to Canada. In 1864 he was nominated for governor by the Ohio Democrats. Running his campaign from Canada, he was defeated. He returned illegally to Ohio in 1865. Mark E. Neeley, Jr., *The Abraham Lincoln Encyclopedia* (New York: McGraw-Hill Book Co., 1982), 317–18.

9. David M. Silver, *Lincoln's Supreme Court* (Urbana: University of Illinois Press, 1957), 84–85, 57.

10. Ibid., 16–18, 20–22.

11. *Detroit Free Press*, February 26, 1864.

12. Kenneth M. Stampp, *Indiana Politics during the Civil War* (Indianapolis: Indiana Historical Bureau, 1949); Emma Lou Thornbrough, *Indiana in the Civil War Era* (Indianapolis: Indiana Historical Bureau and the Indiana Historical Society, 1965); and Gilbert R. Tredway, *Democratic Opposition to the Lincoln Administration in Indiana* (Indianapolis: Indiana Historical Bureau, 1973). These books are the principal sources on which this paper's statements about Indiana politics are based. They are specifically cited only when deemed necessary. See also John D. Barnhart, "The Impact of the Civil War on Indiana," *Indiana Magazine of History* 57 (September 1961):185–224.

13. *Centerville Indiana True Republican*, May 17, 23, 1861.

14. Stampp, *Indiana Politics*, 82, 84.

15. W. H. H. Terrell, *Report of the Adjutant General of the State of Indiana* (Indianapolis: Alexander H. Conner, state printer, 1869), 1:88.

16. Stampp, *Indiana Politics*, 94.

17. George W. Julian, *Political Recollections, 1840–1872* (Chicago: Jansen, McClurg & Co., 1884), 244.

18. Stampp, *Indiana Politics*, 136; *Indianapolis Daily Journal*, June 19, 20, 21, 23, 1862.

19. Terrell, *Report of the Adjutant General*, 1:295. Generally discredited by historians, the grand jury's report states that there were 15,000 members of the Knights of the Golden Circle in Indiana.

20. Stampp, *Indiana Politics*, 151–52. There is an earlier and contrary thesis regarding the dissenting Democrats in 1862 and, for that matter, throughout the war. This thesis contends that the Northern Democrats and dissenters were, in the main, disloyal and committed to the success of the rebellion. See, for example, Leonard Kenworthy, *The Tall Sycamore of the Wabash: Daniel Wolsey Voorhees* (Boston: B. Humphries, 1936); Wood Gray, *The Hidden Civil War: The Story of the Copperheads* (New York: Viking Press, 1942); and George Fort Milton, *Abraham Lincoln and the Fifth Column* (New York: Vanguard Press, 1942). This paper rejects this thesis because those who assert it seem unable to support it with other than Republican allegations.

21. Klement, *Dark Lanterns*, 152.

22. Telegrams Received File, Vol. 4, Part 2, 759, War Department Records, National Archives, Washington, D.C.

23. Ariel and William H. Draper, comps., *Brevier Legislative Reports* (South Bend, 1863), vol. 6. The previously noted books by Stampp, Thornbrough, and Tredway contain good descriptions of the legislative maneuvering. See also Lorna Lutes Sylvester, "Oliver P. Morton and the Indiana Legislature of 1863," in *Their Infinite Variety: Essays on Indiana Politicians* (Indianapolis: Indiana Historical Bureau, 1981), 123–54.

24. Sylvester, "Oliver P. Morton," 123–54; Stampp, *Indiana Politics*, 179ff. For a biographical sketch of Terrell, see "Editorial Note," *Indiana in the War of the Rebellion, Report of the Adjutant General* (Indianapolis: Indiana Historical Bureau, 1960). This volume is a reprint of volume 1 of the eight-volume report prepared by W. H. H. Terrell and published in 1869.

25. Klement, *Dark Lanterns*, chap. 4; Stampp, *Indiana Politics*, chap. 10; Frank L. Klement, "The Indianapolis Treason Trials and Ex Parte Milligan," in *American Political Trials*, ed. Michael Belknap (Westport, Ct.: Greenwood Press, 1981), 107–110.

26. Tredway, *Democratic Opposition*, 225.

27. *Special Orders No. 129, September 17, 1864*, General Courts Martial, Records of the Office of the Judge Advocate General, National Archives, Washington, D.C. At the time of Hovey's appointment, Assistant Adjutant General E. D. Townsend, identifying Secretary Stanton as his authority, told Hovey that he was authorized to make "military arrests" and to organize "courts-martial." Letter of Townsend to Hovey, September 14, 1864, Hovey Manuscripts, Lilly Library, Indiana University, Bloomington. In notes that he wrote in approximately 1882 to be used in his obituary, Hovey credited himself with having "crushed a fearful rebellion" in Indiana by his arrests. Hovey Manuscripts, Lilly Library, Indiana University, Bloomington.

28. The arrests and the individuals arrested are described in Tredway, *Democratic Opposition*, 218–19, and in Klement, "The Indianapolis Treason Trials," 101–127. David T. Yeakel and James B. Wilson were seized on November 5, 1864. Milligan is described in Darwin Kelley, *Milligan's Fight against Lincoln* (New York: Exposition Press, 1973). He is also characterized and discussed in Tredway, *Democratic Opposition*, 155–56, 156–59.

29. Klement, *Dark Lanterns*, 152; Klement, "The Indianapolis Treason Trials," 109.

30. Terrell, *Report of the Adjutant General*, 1:360. This report also appears in *Official Records of the Union and Confederate Armies* (Washington, D.C.: Government Printing Office, 1882–1900), series 2,7:930–53.

31. Tredway, *Democratic Opposition*, 225.

32. *Lawrenceburg Democratic Register*, February 19, 27, 1863; April 15, 1864.

33. *Indianapolis Daily Journal*, October 5, November 3, 16, 1864.

34. Record Group NN2716, Records of the Office of the Judge Advocate General's Office, General Courts' Martial, 1812–1939.

35. Dodd's trial and escape are described and discussed in Tredway, *Democratic Opposition*, 225–26; Stampp, *Indiana Politics*, 247–49; Klement, *Dark Lanterns*, 173–77; Klement, "The Indianapolis Treason Trials," 108–110. See also Report of Judge Advocate General Holt to "The Secretary of War for the President," December 14, 1864, in *Official Records of the Union and Confederate Armies*, series 2, 7:1214–17.

36. Stampp, *Indiana Politics*, 253.

37. Tredway, *Democratic Opposition*, 224–25, 227. Benn Pitman, *The Trials for Treason* (Cincinnati, Ohio: Moore, Wilsatch & Baldwin, 1865), 73.

38. General Court Martial Orders, October 15, 1864, Adjutant General's Papers, Records of the Office of the Judge Advocate General, National Archives, Washington, D.C.

39. The specifications appear in the United States Supreme Court's report of the Milligan case. *Ex parte In the Matter of Lambdin P. Milligan, Petitioner*, December 17, 1866, 71 U.S. (4 Wall.) 2, 18 L. Ed. 281.

40. Tredway, *Democratic Opposition*, 244–45.

41. Testimony of Heffren, Record Group NN3409, Records of the Office of the Judge Advocate General's Office, General Courts' Martial, 1812–1939, MS No. 11: 402–403.

42. Record Group NN3409, Records of the Office of the Judge Advocate General's Office, General Courts' Martial, 1812–1939; Klement, "The Indianapolis Treason Trials," 114; Tredway, *Democratic Opposition*, 249; Kenneth M. Stampp, "The Milligan Case and the Election of 1864 in Indiana," *Mississippi Valley Historical Review* 31 (1944–45): 41.

43. *Huntington Democrat*, June 7, 1866. See Kelley, *Milligan's Fight against Lincoln*, 95–96. Col. Reuben Williams, another commissioner, later recalled that "the testimony . . . was so convincing that there was not a dissenting vote on the first ballot. . . ." *Warsaw Times*, quoted in *Indianapolis Daily Journal*, January 8, 1900.

44. Kelley, *Milligan's Fight against Lincoln*, 96. Kelley quotes a letter from Justice David Davis to William H. Herndon citing McDonald's intervention.

45. President Andrew Johnson to General Hovey, May 16, 1865, *Official Records of the Union and Confederate Armies*, series 2, 8:587.

46. Governor Morton to President Johnson, May 24, 1865, Record Group NN3409, Records of the Judge Advocate General, General Courts' Martial, 1812–1839, Box 1164; William D. Foulke, *Life of Oliver P. Morton: Including His Important Speeches* (2 vols. Indianapolis-Kansas City: Bowen-Merrill Co., 1899), 1:428–31.

47. Secretary Stanton to General Hovey, May 30, 1865, *Official Records of the Union and Confederate Armies*, series 2, 8:583–84, 637.

48. The facts regarding this proceeding are taken from the United States Supreme Court report of the Milligan case, *Ex parte In the Matter of Lambdin P. Milligan, Petitioner*, December 17, 1866, 71 U.S. (4 Wall.) 2, 18 L. Ed. 281.

49. This legislation is set forth in the United States Supreme Court's report. Lincoln's proclamation appears in *Collected Works*, 6:451.

50. *Ex parte Milligan*, 18 L. Ed. 281, 291.

51. Silver, *Lincoln's Supreme Court*, 203, 205.

52. *Encyclopedia Brittanica*, s.v. "Field, David Dudley," "Garfield, James A.," "Black, Jeremiah S.," and "Butler, Benjamin F."

53. The first concerned the authority of the circuit court in Indianapolis to certify the three questions. If the circuit court had no such authority, the Supreme Court would not have had the jurisdiction to hear and decide the three questions. The opinion rejected this defense. The government then argued that the case was moot, that is, that it was no longer pending for decision because the record did not show that Milligan was still alive and it was legally

presumed that he had been hanged. The opinion rather crisply rejected this contention. All quotations from the following opinions can be found in *Ex parte Milligan*, 18 L. Ed. 281, 295–302.

54. Ralph D. Gray, ed., *Gentlemen from Indiana* (Indianapolis: Indiana Historical Bureau, 1977), 119–39. Gray wrote the essay concerning Hendricks.

55. The file of this case, variously captioned as *Lambdin P. Milligan* v. *James R. Slack and Others* and *Lambdin P. Milligan* v. *Alvin P. Hovey and Others*, is identified as Case No. 142, Federal Records Center, Chicago. It is discussed in Tredway, *Democratic Opposition*, 257–62, and Klement, "The Indianapolis Treason Trials and Ex Parte Milligan," in *American Political Trials*, ed. Michael Belknap, chap. 5:119.

56. Stampp, *Indiana Politics during the Civil War*; Klement, *Dark Lanterns*; Klement, "The Indianapolis Treason Trials and Ex Parte Milligan," in *American Political Trials*, ed. Michael Belknap, chap. 5; Frank L. Klement, *The Copperheads in the Middle West* (Chicago: University of Chicago Press, 1960), 192–99.

57. Stampp and Klement discuss the societies and the Northwest Conspiracy, but Tredway's examination in *Democratic Opposition*, chaps. 7, 8, 9, and 10, is the most comprehensive. For an excellent survey of the literature and scholarship about "Copperheads," see Richard O. Curry, "The Union as It Was: A Critique of Recent Interpretations of the Copperheads," *Civil War History* 13 (March 1967):25.

58. Terrell, *Report of the Adjutant General of the State of Indiana*, 1:231, 232, 233.

59. *The Statistical History of the United States, from Colonial Times to the Present* (Stamford, Ct.: Fairfield Publishers, Inc., 1965), 688.

60. William F. Fox, *Regimental Losses in the American Civil War* (Albany: Albany Publishing Co., 1889), 532–36. Fox also made a complex adjustment to exclude black troops and certain others and to convert the data to the standard of a three-year enlistment. On this basis he ranked Kansas first and Indiana second in terms of the participation of the percentage of military population.

61. Terrell, *Report of the Adjutant General of the State of Indiana*, 1:248. Terrell states that only 17,899 men were drafted in Indiana throughout the war.

62. Tredway, *Democratic Opposition*, 60–62, and congressional district map facing page 225. The first district included the "pocket" counties, Vanderburgh and the southwest corner of the state; the second included Clark and Floyd counties and the southeast corner; and the seventh centered around Vigo and Sullivan counties.

63. 18 L. Ed. 296.

The Kinsey Customs Case and Constitutional Law

Kenneth R. Stevens

Mr. Stevens is Assistant Professor of History, Texas Christian University. He is the author of "United States v. 31 Photographs: Dr. Alfred C. Kinsey and Obscenity Law," Indiana Magazine of History.

In 1950, when Alfred C. Kinsey began to import erotic materials for study at his Indiana University Institute for Sex Research, he quickly ran up against federal obscenity statutes of his day. A lengthy, complicated, and expensive legal case ensued between Kinsey and the United States government. The institute eventually won its case in 1957, but that was some months after Kinsey's death. In the Kinsey decision—known officially as *United States* v. *31 Photographs*—a federal court granted scientists at the Institute for Sex Research the right to import and study materials which under ordinary circumstances would be considered obscene.[1] In so doing the case helped establish an important standard in the field of censorship law: the concept of "variable obscenity," based on the premise that obscenity is not absolute but varies according to the nature of the audience or receiving group.

Viewed from the perspective of 1985, it is difficult to understand what all the excitement was about. Materials involved in the Kinsey case included some erotic photographs, several French postcards featuring women in various stages of undress, drawings by the Belgian artist Félicien Rops, and sexually explicit books, most notably the Marquis de Sade's *Les 120 Journées de Sodome*. Unquestionably every item in the case had erotic content. Yet by the standards of today, these materials were tame indeed. In 1985 sexually explicit literature is available not only in adult bookstores, but in the neighborhood grocery. The two top-selling "men's interests" magazines, *Playboy* and *Penthouse*, have a combined circulation of about seven-and-a-half million copies per issue, approximately the same as the combined circulation of the top national news magazines in the country, *Time* and *Newsweek*.[2]

Playboy Corporation, in fact, has created its own cable television network, on which viewers can watch films such as *Lonely Wives* ("married women seek ways to occupy themselves while their husbands are away"), *Wanda Whips Wall Street* ("marginal stockbrokers improve their performance when maneuvered by bullish woman"), and *Ultra Flesh* ("futuristic female recharges rundown parts").[3] Movies that are primarily sexual in content are not restricted to the Playboy Channel, however. More family-oriented cable networks, such as Showtime and Home Box Office, have late evening "softcore" films in which nudity and sex are far more important than plot.

Perhaps the ultimate symbol of the striking evolution in American sexual mores over the years can be seen in the 1984 Miss America fiasco. Although denounced as exploitive by many, the Miss American Pageant has always represented itself as a celebration of the ideal American woman—talented, beautiful, and perhaps above all, wholesome. The winner of the 1984 contest, Vanessa Williams, was forced to resign her title after revelations that she had posed for photographs depicting lesbian sexual activity. The most interesting aspect of this affair was the degree to which the public rallied to her defense. In one admittedly unscientific poll conducted by the *Los Angeles Herald-Examiner*, 65 percent of the respondents felt Ms. Williams should have retained her title.[4] Truly the standards of what is permissible have changed greatly in the years since Alfred Kinsey tried to import thirty-one erotic photographs. To understand how Kinsey could get into so much trouble, we need to look at his career as a sex researcher and at the state of federal obscenity law at that time.

Alfred C. Kinsey grew up in the New York suburb of South Orange, New Jersey. His father, an engineering professor at the Stevens Institute of Technology in nearby Hoboken, desired his son to follow in his footsteps. Alfred dutifully enrolled at Stevens Tech after high school graduation in 1912, even though he disliked engineering. After two years at the school, he could stand no more. Disregarding his father's wishes, Kinsey transferred to Bowdoin College, from which he graduated in 1916 with a degree in his favorite subject—biology. That fall he began graduate studies at Harvard, and upon completion of his doctoral degree, he accepted a position as an assistant professor of biology at Indiana University.[5]

Remembering Kinsey today, it is difficult to think of him except as a person of great controversy, but the fact is that for the eighteen-year period from 1920 to 1938, he had a rather ordinary academic career at Indiana University. He married and had children, built a house, participated in a faculty discussion group, and worried about campus politics. He enjoyed a solid reputation as a scholar, recognized internationally in academic circles for his research on the gall wasp and other insects. Those who knew him said that he taught effectively, that he cared for and respected his students, and that they returned his affection.[6]

Then his life changed dramatically. In 1938 the university began a new interdisciplinary course on marriage. Kinsey was selected to direct the course, which was designed to cover the whole range of married life, including legal aspects, economics, ethics, and most significantly for Kinsey, biology.

Given his natural curiosity, participation in the marriage course developed Kinsey's interest in sexual behavior, and he took a bold— and perhaps unwarranted—step. He began taking sexual histories from the students. The more Kinsey recorded, the more he became convinced of a startling realization: very little accurate scientific information existed regarding human sexual behavior. Within a few months Kinsey had in mind the outline of a great project to study the entire range of human sexual experience. Controversy erupted. Some of Kinsey's colleagues questioned his activities. Bloomington religious leaders pressured university president Herman B Wells about the professor. Wells offered Kinsey a choice: he could continue teaching and give up sex research, or he could continue his research under the auspices of the university and give up teaching in the marriage course. But he could not do both. Kinsey's decision was difficult but inevitable. The research continued.[7]

By 1950 Kinsey's reputation as a sex researcher was well established. Along with his associates at what was now called the Indiana University Institute for Sex Research, he had collected thousands of sex histories. The institute's monumental *Sexual Behavior in the Human Male* was published in 1948, and work on the companion female volume was well underway.[8]

As the work progressed, one subject that came to intrigue Kinsey was the nature of the relationship between art and the erotic. He believed that explaining that relationship would provide one key to understanding the place of erotica in our culture. He also hoped to publish a comparative study of western and oriental erotic art which would examine attitudes toward sex in different cultures.[9] In the course of his research, Kinsey began to collect erotic and pornographic items for the institute's library. Most of them came from overseas, and their importation soon brought Kinsey into conflict with the law.

The main problem facing the professor was the current legal definition of obscenity. The 1930 tariff act prohibited the importation of obscenity, and Kinsey soon found that the materials he wished to acquire were prohibited. At that time the leading precedent in censorship law was an 1868 English decision, *Queen* v. *Hicklin*. The case arose from the publication of *The Confessional Unmasked . . .*, a virulently anti-Catholic pamphlet which impugned the morality of the priesthood. Only a portion of the pamphlet dealt with sexual matters, but in ruling against it the Queen's chief justice held that writing could be declared obscene on the basis of select passages in the work and that the test of obscenity could be determined by "whether the tendency of the matter" was to "deprave and corrupt those whose minds are open to such immoral influences" and into whose hands it might fall.[10]

It was an important decision. According to the Hicklin rule the possible objectionable effects of isolated passages upon susceptible individuals—such as children or hopeless neurotics—could result in works of substantial literary value being declared obscene if they contained any sexual references. And such frequently was the case. In 1873 Congress passed a law banning obscenity from the United States mail; subsequently the 1930 federal tariff act prohibited its importation. In both instances the Hicklin standard served as a guide for the courts.[11]

Over the years some relaxation in the law occurred. In 1933 the well-known New York censorship lawyer Morris L. Ernst successfully defended James Joyce's novel *Ulysses* against obscenity charges which prohibited that book's importation under the tariff act.[12] But such concessions were allowed only to works of clear artistic and literary merit. When Kinsey attempted to import erotic materials of no substantial literary or artistic value, he ran squarely afoul standards of obscenity law established in the Victorian era.

For a time Kinsey was the beneficiary of an informal understanding with the Indianapolis Customs Bureau, which allowed him to receive his shipments. But in 1950 the local office requested official guidance from Washington regarding the institute's imports. The response from the assistant commissioner of customs was emphatic. Everything submitted for examination by the Indianapolis bureau, he declared, was "grossly obscene." The most liberal interpretation of federal obscenity standards could not bring them within the guidelines of the tariff act.[13] Clearly the ruling was a serious setback for Kinsey. In order to continue his research, he had to reach some understanding with the Customs Bureau.

For some time Kinsey had been aware of Morris Ernst's legal reputation, and the two had corresponded on the subject of censorship over the years. When he learned of the government's decision regarding his imports, Kinsey contacted the defender of *Ulysses*. Ernst felt that one possibility existed for an easy settlement of the customs difficulty. The tariff act of 1930 did allow the secretary of the treasury to grant administrative exceptions to the law for works of "established literary or scientific merit." This discretionary authority was the basis on which Ernst had won the admission of *Ulysses* into the country in 1933. Kinsey's materials were questionable in nature, but it could be argued that the scientific significance of his research entitled him to an administrative exception from the secretary. Working with Ernst and Ernst's law partner, Harriet Pilpel, Kinsey agreed to pursue this route. His desire was not to be involved in any landmark legal dispute, but simply to clear the way for his research as quickly as possible.

In June, 1950, Pilpel and Kinsey met with the Customs Bureau's legal adviser in Washington to argue that the professor should receive a discretionary exception to the tariff act. Pilpel conceded that many of Kinsey's importations were patently obscene, but, she argued, he had to have access to them in order to carry out research that would be of genuine scientific significance. Obviously, she maintained, "many works of great merit would be impossible if their authors were not permitted access to raw material."[14]

The government response was disappointing. Kinsey was informed that "established scientific merit" as specified in the tariff act was not the same as "scientific significance." Any exception to the law for Kinsey would have to be declared by the federal courts.[15]

Blocked in the attempt to reach an administrative understanding, Kinsey reluctantly agreed to a legal test. Although he regretted the time and expense of a court fight, he informed Pilpel that he was "increasingly convinced that we should push this until we have clearly established our right to import any kind of sexual material."[16]

About this time Kinsey's legal difficulties began to attract nationwide attention. In November, 1950, with shipments valued at nearly $3,000 in transit from overseas, newspapers discovered the Kinsey controversy. On November 17 and 18, Indianapolis newspapers carried front-page stories about the customs dispute. A few days later the local customs office seized yet another Kinsey shipment, which one official described as "so obscene that any scientific value is lost." The Associated Press and United Press International wire services picked up the story, and Kinsey began to draw editorial fire around the country. One newspaper remarked that Kinsey's "pictures of moral degenerates in degenerate poses" could not reveal much of scientific worth.[17]

The news hardly could have broken at a worse time. With record appropriations for the state universities pending before the Indiana legislature, Gov. Henry F. Schricker feared a political backlash over the Kinsey affair. He placed an angry telephone call to university president Herman Wells about the matter. Kinsey, too, was upset by the unfavorable publicity. Besieged by reporters, he was described by the *Indianapolis Star* as "touchy and irritable on the whole subject." In response to inquiries about the customs problem, the professor issued a press release. It read in part:

> The Institute for Sex Research, at Indiana University, explains that it has inevitably had to gather data and materials which, under other circumstances and in other places, would be considered obscene. . . .
> The Institute feels that the issue is much broader than that of the importation of a specific object at a given time and place. It considers that the issue is one which concerns all scholars who need access to so-called obscene materials for scientific investigations which in the long run may contribute to human welfare.[18]

Alongside the newspaper episode, Kinsey's lawyers continued their efforts in the legal case. Their plan called for obviously pornographic materials to be sent to the institute through the federal customs office in New York. The collector there agreed to seize the shipments for violation of the tariff act, and the federal attorney at New York promised to initiate proceedings. To start the process Kinsey ordered several items from overseas, including de Sade's *Les 120 Journées de Sodome* and several drawings by Félicien Rops. Subsequently, he placed additional orders with a Copenhagen bookstore, informing his supplier that he needed "the most openly erotic material" available. In response the bookdealer prepared a varied collection, which he sent to Kinsey in several small packages. One of the shipments included thirty-one photographs, which he described as "the most openly erotic . . . anyone could imagine—and rather pretty," too. Ironically, several of the packages passed through New York customs unchallenged and had to be returned to the collector for re-examination. In the end, Kinsey's lawyers and the Customs Bureau agreed on a number of items—including the thirty-one photo-graphs—which would be charged with obscenity for the court test.[19]

Although they had completed the groundwork for the legal case, Kinsey's attorneys still had not abandoned hope of reaching an administrative agreement with the government. In May, 1953, Harriet Pilpel met once more with a Treasury Department lawyer to ask that Kinsey be granted a discretionary exception to the tariff law.[20] The request was duly taken into the maze of government bureau-cracy, not to be seen again for almost three years, when it was denied.

Meanwhile, in September, 1953, the institute published its second book, *Sexual Behavior in the Human Female*. Within ten days the book went into six printings, bringing even more attention and criticism to Kinsey and Indiana University. Congressman Louis B. Heller of New York proposed that the book be banned from the mails until Congress could investigate. And it was rumored that the Special House Committee on Tax-Exempt Foundations also intended to examine the institute.[21] In the face of mounting hostility and pres-sure against the institute's work, one of its main financial supporters, the Rockefeller Foundation, wavered and finally withdrew its fund-ing. It was a hard time for the Institute for Sex Research on many fronts.

The legal battle, however, moved slowly. Although the government retained possession of institute imports seized as early as 1950, no charges were filed until the summer of 1956. The problem was partly government inertia and partly the tactics adopted by Kinsey's law-yers, who still sought an administrative exception to the tariff law in order to avoid the risk of a court fight. Meanwhile the seized ma-terials remained in federal custody. While a six-year delay is not extraordinary in either legal or government circles, it must have been agonizing for Kinsey, who was becoming increasingly aware of his own mortality.

By this time Alfred Kinsey was a desperately ill man. After suf-fering a number of small heart attacks, he learned through a physical examination that his heart was enlarged. His doctor ordered him to reduce his workday to no more than four hours, but Kinsey refused. In June he wrote Harriet Pilpel: "I have been more or less continuously in bed, in the hospital and at home, for the last three weeks. It is this heart again, and it impresses me with the importance of getting our business done systematically while I can still keep at it."[22] But his time ran out. On August 25, 1956, Kinsey died at Bloomington Hospital.

The customs case outlived Kinsey by more than a year. On July 16, 1957, Pilpel, on behalf of the institute, and United States Attorney Benjamin Richards, representing the government, presented their arguments before Judge Edmund L. Palmieri of the Southern District of New York federal court.[23] To save time and further expense, both sides agreed to waive their rights to jury trial and asked the court to issue a judgment from the bench. In her remarks Pilpel defended the standing of Kinsey and his research facility in the academic community. She explained the careful conditions under which erotic materials at the institute were supervised. She also stressed the importance of the detained materials to Kinsey's research. Historically, she maintained, privileged exceptions to the tariff law had been allowed by the courts in cases of conscientious and qualified individuals. In 1936, for example, in *United States* v. *One Package*, a federal court had upheld the right of a physician to import contraceptives even though they would normally be banned under the tariff act.[24] The same logic could be applied to Kinsey's importations.

In her main constitutional point, Kinsey's lawyer argued that obscenity was not an absolute concept, but relative, or variable, depending on circumstances. As a precedent she cited the case of *United States* v. *Levine*.[25] Esar Levine had been charged with mailing obscene advertisements for a number of books, including *The Secret Museum of Anthropology*, a photographic collection of nudes from around the world, and *Crossways of Sex*, which promised readers details of the "weirdest passions and perversions ever recorded." Levine, however, promised more than he delivered. In the case Judge Learned Hand, of the Second Circuit Court of Appeals, ruled that while Levine's wares might be injurious to young children, they were so innocuous that they could not be considered obscene from an adult perspective. Obscenity, Hand declared, was not absolute, but a "function of many variables," including the nature of the audience. Pilpel contended that as qualified scientists, the researchers of Kinsey's institute were an audience which would not be sexually disturbed by erotic materials.

In rebuttal, Richards disputed Pilpel's claims. In the government's view there was no legitimate comparison between the contraceptives at issue in the *One Package* decision and the things Kinsey sought to import. Kinsey's materials were plainly obscene. He denied that any provision in the law distinguished the character of the audience and, for that matter, that scientists possessed any special immunity to the effects of pornography.[26]

Three months later, in October, 1957, Judge Palmieri handed down a decision in favor of the institute's right to import erotic materials.[27] He based his judgment partly on Pilpel's arguments and partly on a major Supreme Court case, *Roth* v. *United States*, decided earlier that year.[28] Samuel Roth, a well-known New York literary pirate and "soft-core" pornography merchant, had been indicted for mailing obscene books and photographs. A jury found Roth guilty, and the trial judge sentenced him to five years in prison with a $5,000 fine. Roth appealed to the Supreme Court, arguing that the federal prohibition against obscenity in the mail violated his First Amendment right of free speech. The Court rejected Roth's appeal, but in doing so it set forth some important guidelines for obscenity law. According to the Roth ruling, the test of obscenity was to determine whether, in applying the contemporary standards of the average person in the community, the dominant theme of the material appealed to prurient interest.

In Kinsey's case, Judge Palmieri ruled that the staff of the Institute for Sex Research was not made up of average persons, but of scholars who examined erotic materials only for the purposes of scientific research. The material was not likely to appeal to their prurient interest, and it was carefully restricted from the general public, which could be affected adversely. He therefore ruled that the detained importations should be released. The Kinsey Institute had won the right to import pornography.

In any immediate sense the decision was a hollow victory. Kinsey was dead, and undoubtedly the strain of the customs case contributed to his end. Attorney fees for the case had cost the institute more than $10,000.[29] The research time lost, which could have been devoted to important—and still unanswered—questions, such as the influence of pornography on sex offenders, was incalculable.

But the Kinsey case also has a larger constitutional dimension. In holding that certain scholars could view or read obscene materials without appeal to prurient interest, the Kinsey case reinforced the constitutional doctrine of variable obscenity spelled out earlier in the Levine decision. Much depended on the character of the audience or "receiving group." Harriet Pilpel saw Judge Palmieri's ruling as a reaffirmation of academic freedom, allowing legitimate scholars to study materials that would be considered obscene for the general public.[30]

Other legal writers were more reserved. One commentator warned that "spurious institutes for sex research . . . operating under the pretense of scientific inquiry" might use the Kinsey precedent as legal justification for trafficking in pornography. Another, writing in the *Indiana Law Journal*, pointed out that the variable concept of *31 Photographs* introduced a number of practical problems in administration and enforcement regarding the character of the receiving group.[31] How could it be possible to determine beforehand whether a particular audience would be offended by any particular materials?

Despite these understandable objections, two prominent constitutional scholars, William B. Lockhart and Robert C. McClure, have urged courts to adopt the variable standard. In their view it provides the most practical test of obscenity for a society that desires to provide "maximum freedom for willing readers or viewers with a desire to protect the sensibilities of those who wish to avoid objectionable materials."[32] Implicit in the variable concept is a recognition that American society is not homogeneous, that materials which might offend a thirteen-year-old or particular individuals within the adult population might not offend the entire adult population.

Thus, under the variable concept the Supreme Court could determine as it did in 1968 that in selling so-called "girlie" magazines to minors under age seventeen, Long Island luncheonette owner Sam Ginsburg had violated obscenity standards for that audience, even though the same magazines earlier had been declared not obscene for an adult audience.[33]

The variable concept, growing out of the Kinsey decision and similar cases preceding it (such as *U.S. v. Levine*), has had a significant impact on the development of American obscenity law. *Thirty-One Photographs* was directly cited in the 1966 Supreme Court decision upholding the conviction of *Eros* publisher Ralph Ginzburg, who had used the mails to advertise his sexually explicit books and magazines.[34] In his opinion Justice William Brennan noted the contrast between Ginzburg's "pandering" and the scientific purposes of the individuals involved in the Kinsey case. The concept of variable obscenity, though without direct reference to *31 Photographs*, was also employed in several other Supreme Court decisions during the 1960s.[35]

But the Roth decision—used by Judge Palmieri—was a hydra-headed precedent. The same case that could be used to distinguish between scientists and the hypothetical "average person" provided the rather vague concept of contemporary community standards. In 1973, in *Miller v. California*, the Supreme Court waded into these murky waters when it held that Miller had violated the community standards of Orange County, California, by mailing unsolicited materials such as *Sex Orgies Illustrated* to random addressees. The decision in the case returned to the notion that certain materials are "hard-core" pornography, inherently obscene, no matter what the character of the audience.[36] As a result the old issue of defining obscenity in absolute terms had again to be addressed. It was this very dilemma that a decade before had caused Justice Potter Stewart to declare in exasperation, "I can't define it, but I know it when I see it."[37]

The concepts of contemporary community standards and hard-core pornography have not resolved the obscenity problem. Defining "pornography" and even "community" is a difficult proposition. Too loose a standard may subject members of the community to material they find objectionable, while too strict a standard censors materials from those less easily offended. It may be that defining obscenity is an impossible task to expect of the legal system. Still, it can be argued that the variable concept is a better choice than the absolute standard followed by the courts since the Miller decision.

Our real difficulty in dealing with obscenity is that we rely on the law to resolve a problem that is largely social. And pornography is undeniably a serious social problem, whether in terms of the growing trend toward violence in pornographic materials, the tragic increase in child pornography, or the expansion of pornography outlets from the underground to Main Street, where it finds the general public rather than the interested audience seeking it out.

In the broadest perspective, Alfred C. Kinsey was trying to deal with these forces within our society. His work was not the cause nor even a contributor to the problem of obscenity; he was trying to understand it and explain it. It is ironic and unfortunate that his efforts were blocked by a legal system that, in trying to protect us all, thwarted those who could have helped.

Notes

1. *U.S. v. 31 Photographs*, 156 F. Supp. 350 (1957).

2. *The 1984 IMS/Ayer Directory of Publications* (Fort Washington, Pa.: IMS Press, 1984). The figures are: *Playboy*, 4,250,324; *Penthouse*, 3,453,713; *Time*, 4,719,343; *Newsweek*, 3,022,727.

3. *Cable Connection*, October 14, 1984, 30.

4. *Newsweek*, August 6, 1984, 23.

5. Wardell B. Pomeroy, *Dr. Kinsey and the Institute for Sex Research* (New York: New American Library, 1973), 33–46.

6. Ibid., 46–60.

7. Ibid., 61–70; James H. Jones, "The Origins of the Institute for Sex Research: A History" (Ph.D. diss., Indiana University, 1972), 81–161. Jones maintains that Kinsey "intended to use the Marriage Course to launch a major study of human sexual behavior" from the beginning. He estimates that it had taken Kinsey months, possibly a full year before the Marriage Course began, to prepare the questionnaire he gave to his students (p. 98).

8. Alfred C. Kinsey, Wardell B. Pomeroy, and Clyde Martin, *Sexual Behavior in the Human Male* (Philadelphia: W. B. Saunders, 1948).

9. Pomeroy, *Kinsey*, 446–47.

10. U.S. Stats., Vol. 46, part 1, title 3, 688–89; *Queen v. Hicklin*, 3 Q.B. 360 (1868). The text of the decision is in Edward De Grazia, comp., *Censorship Landmarks* (New York: R. R. Bowker, 1969), 5–11.

11. 18 United States Code, sect. 1461; U.S. Stats., Vol. 46, part 1, title 3, 688–89.

12. *U.S. v. Ulysses*, 5 F. Supp. 182 (1933); Kenneth R. Stevens, "*Ulysses* on Trial," *Library Chronicle* 20/21 (1982): 91–105.

13. Assistant Commissioner of Customs David B. Strubinger to Indianapolis Collector Alden H. Baker, May 29, 1950, Institute for Sex Research Papers, Indiana University, Bloomington (hereafter ISRP).

14. Harriet Pilpel to Huntington Cairns, June 20, 1950, ISRP.

15. Walter R. Johnson to Kinsey, June 27, 1950; Harriet Pilpel, "Memo re Conference with Messrs. Johnson and Cairns on Friday afternoon, September 15, 1950, at Mr. Cairns's office in Washington," both in ISRP.

16. Kinsey to Pilpel, September 22, 1950, ISRP.

17. Clippings from the *Indianapolis Star*, November 17, 1950; *Indianapolis News*, November 17, 1950; *Indianapolis Times*, November 17, 1950; *Bloomington (Indiana) Herald-Telephone*, November 25, 1950; *Anniston (Alabama) Star*, November 29, 1950, all in ISRP.

18. Author's interview with Herman B Wells, November 20, 1973; clipping from *Indianapolis Star*, November 17, 1950; Alfred C. Kinsey, "Press Release," November 17, 1950, ISRP.

19. Harriet Pilpel to Kinsey, October 3, 1950; Pilpel to Kinsey, October 5, 1950; Kinsey to Pilpel, January 16, 1951; Pilpel to Kinsey, January 22, 1951; Kinsey to Philobiblon, March 22, 1951; Philobiblon to Kinsey, April 4, 1951; Pilpel to Kinsey, May 14, 1951; Pilpel to Kinsey, May 31, 1951, all letters in ISRP.

20. Pilpel to Charles R. McNeill, May 14, 1953, ISRP.

21. Cornelia V. Christenson, *Kinsey: A Biography* (Bloomington: Indiana University Press, 1971), 158ff.; Alfred C. Kinsey, Wardell Pomeroy, Clyde Martin, and Paul H. Gebhard, *Sexual Behavior in the Human Female* (Philadelphia: W. B. Saunders, 1953).

22. Kinsey to Pilpel, June 26, 1956, ISRP.

23. "*U.S.* v. *31 Photographs*: Brief in Support of Motion for Summary Judgment of the Claimant," ISRP; "*U.S.* v. *31 Photographs*: Libellant's Memorandum of Law upon Cross-Motions for Summary Judgment," Barnes, Hickham, Pantzer and Boyd law office, Indianapolis.

24. *U.S.* v. *One Package*, 86 F. 2d 737 (1936).

25. *U.S.* v. *Levine*, 86 F. 2d 156 (1936).

26. Benjamin T. Richards to Edmund L. Palmieri, October 14, 1957, ISRP.

27. "*U.S.* v. *31 Photographs*: Decision in Support of Summary Judgment for the Claimant, the Institute for Sex Research at Indiana University," ISRP.

28. *Roth* v. *U.S.*, 354 U.S. 476, 489 (1957).

29. Morris L. Ernst and Harriet Pilpel calculated the legal fees in the case at $22,070 and invited the institute to make whatever payment it could. Paul H. Gebhard, who took charge of the institute after Kinsey's death, suggested one-half that amount, to which the lawyers agreed. Gebhard to Pilpel, September 19, 1957, ISRP.

30. Harriet Pilpel, "But Can You Do That?" *Publisher's Weekly*, November 25, 1957, 27–28.

31. Ralph E. Pratt, "Case Notes: Obscenity," *Kansas Law Review* 7 (1958): 216–19; unsigned Note in *Indiana Law Journal* 34 (1959): 426–41.

32. William B. Lockhart and Robert C. McClure, "Censorship of Obscenity: The Developing Constitutional Standard," *Minnesota Law Review* 45 (1960): 1–121, esp. 68–88; Frederick Schauer, *The Law of Obscenity* (Washington, D.C.: Bureau of National Affairs, 1976), 94.

33. *Ginsburg* v. *New York*, 390 U.S. 629 (1968).

34. *Ginzburg* v. *U.S.*, 383 U.S. 463 (1966).

35. See, for example, *U.S.* v. *Klaw*, 350 F. 2d 155 (1965) and *Mishkin* v. *New York*, 383 U.S. 502 (1968).

36. *Miller* v. *California*, 413 U.S. 15 (1973).

37. *Jacobellis* v. *Ohio*, 378 U.S. 184 (1964).

The Indianapolis
School Busing Case

Emma Lou Thornbrough

*Miss Thornbrough is Professor Emeritus, Butler University. Among
her publications are* The Negro in Indiana before 1900 *and* Indiana
in the Civil War Era.

T he title of my talk tonight is "The Indianapolis School Busing
Case." This title would have puzzled our forefathers. Today
the words "bus" and "busing" are among the more pejorative
and emotion-laden in the American-English language, but these
unfavorable connotations are a fairly recent development.

I am interested in tracing the origin and history of words. So I
looked up "bus" and "busing" in a number of dictionaries of different
periods and found pretty much what I expected. The *Century English
Dictionary* (6 vols., 1889) defines *bus* or *buss* as an abbreviation for
omnibus (which, in Latin, of course, means "for everybody")—a collo-
quium for a public street carriage. This sort of definition continued
for several decades in a variety of dictionaries. Bus was always a noun
(never a verb). There was a continuing debate over whether the word
should be spelled with a single or double *s* and whether, as an
abbreviation for omnibus, it should be preceded by an apostrophe
('bus). An *American Usage Dictionary* published in 1957 decided that
"bus" was "sufficiently well established to require no apostrophe."

Finally, in the *Harper Dictionary of Contemporary Usage*, published in
the United States in 1975, I found the following:

> busing/bussing
> As a result of the attempts toward racial integration of the nation's
> schools, the practice of transporting pupils by bus became the center
> of controversy in many communities. Thus the word *busing* appeared
> in headlines across the nation. . . .

By the time of the publication of that dictionary, the threat of
busing for purposes of school desegregation was very much a reality
in Indianapolis.

Thus the yellow school bus—hitherto the symbol of progress and
improved educational opportunity when it was used to transport
rural children to consolidated schools and suburban children to
schools with superior facilities—now became the symbol and code
word for racial fears and stereotypes. A fascinating psychological
phenomenon. But it is not about the psychological aspects of busing

that I shall be talking tonight. This lecture is part of a series on "Indiana and the United States Constitution," so my emphasis will be on constitutional and legal aspects of the Indianapolis school busing case.

At the outset I must confess that I volunteered to do what I am attempting tonight. When the committee was planning the lectures and discussing possible subjects, I announced that I would give this lecture—and now I wonder at my temerity. I was an interested observer of the developments about which I shall be speaking; my research is even mentioned in the footnotes of the District Court's initial decision in 1971. I had a general familiarity with the case. I knew what the main issues were, that it was important, and that several things distinguished it from other school desegregation cases in the North. But after I began my research in earnest I soon recognized that my principal task was going to be to try to sort out the significant issues and developments from the maze of legal motions, appeals, stays, etc., and present them in a way which would make sense to my audience. At the same time I wished to clear up some of the widespread misunderstanding and confusion over the case. (I myself, of course, am not a lawyer.) Since this lecture is in observance of the bicentennial of the U.S. Constitution I shall try to stick as closely as possible to constitutional and legal questions and omit the personalities and politics and human elements with which I could enliven it if time permitted.

Nevertheless, I am not narrating mere cold legal facts and theories. This is a very human drama which affected and continues to affect the lives of many people in the Indianapolis community. We are dealing here with a drama with a large and changing cast of characters as well as changing legal issues. There were changes in the parties to the case. It was brought originally against the Indianapolis Board of School Commissioners, but the defendants were later increased to include suburban school districts outside of Indianapolis and officers of the state of Indiana. The suit was brought originally by the U.S. Department of Justice, but later other plaintiffs entered the case, and the position of the Justice Department shifted and fluctuated, as we shall see. Of course the personnel of the various government units involved change, although in most cases the positions with regard to the suit did not. But significant changes in the membership of the Indianapolis school board finally resulted in IPS

(I shall use IPS instead of constantly repeating Indianapolis Public Schools) asking to change from the position of defendant to plaintiff, a request which was rejected. There were changes in the attorneys in the case; so numerous were the defendants that a large part of the legal talent in Indianapolis was involved. The one individual who played a consistent role in the long and tortuous drama was the judge of the U.S. Court for the Southern District of Indiana, S. Hugh Dillin. I shall mention his name many times, but since the events which I shall recount are so recent and frequently tinged with politics and since some of the individuals currently hold political office, I shall on the whole refrain from the use of personal names.

A little historical background is necessary. As most of us in this audience know, Indiana has had a long history of racial discrimination and legalized segregation. Before 1949 state law permitted, though it did not require, school corporations to maintain segregated schools. In Indianapolis, most, though not all, elementary schools were racially segregated. The high schools were totally segregated. All black students, regardless of their places of residence, were required to attend Crispus Attucks High School, which was opened in 1927. A 1935 state law required the Indianapolis school board to furnish transportation (i.e. busing) for students who attended segregated schools.[1]

In 1949 the state legislature passed a law which declared it to be public policy to provide "equal, non-segregated, non discriminatory educational opportunities and facilities for all, regardless of race, creed, national origin, color, or sex" and "to eliminate and prohibit" segregated schools from kindergarten to state universities. The law provided that no more segregated schools should be constructed and that, beginning in September, 1949, all pupils entering elementary schools or the first year of junior or senior high school were to be enrolled in the school in the district where they lived without regard to race.[2]

The Indianapolis school authorities had lobbied for years against the adoption of anti-segregation legislation, and while the adoption of the 1949 law was pending, the Indianapolis branch of the National Association for the Advancement of Colored People released a survey of school construction plans, charging that the board was "over-building" Negro schools in anticipation of the adoption of the new law. Nevertheless, in April, 1949, the school board announced its intention of compliance. Separate school districts for white and Negro pupils were to be abolished. By 1953 school authorities announced that the program of desegregation had been completed in the high schools and that the first so-called "integrated" classes would graduate the following year.

It should be noted that the adoption of the desegregation law and the steps taken to comply with it occurred before 1954, when in *Brown* v. *Board of Education* the United States Supreme Court unanimously held that the doctrine of "separate but equal" had no place in public education and that segregation supported by law was a violation of the Equal Protection Clause of the Fourteenth Amendment.[3]

Ten years later Congress took a step intended primarily to accelerate the process of desegregation in public schools in the South but which became the basis for the suit against the Indianapolis schools when it passed the Civil Rights Act of 1964.

By the 1960s, a period when there was growing awareness of and sensitivity to racial discrimination, when the civil rights protests were at their peak, and when the Indiana state legislature as well as Congress passed significant civil rights legislation, there was increasing criticism that Indianapolis school authorities were violating the spirit of the 1949 school law and were, in fact, following policies and adopting measures intended to perpetuate rather than eliminate racial segregation. As late as 1964 neither Broad Ripple nor Northwest High School enrolled a single black student, while there was not a single white student at Attucks. Little had been done to integrate teaching and administrative staffs. White teachers taught at predominantly white schools; black teachers, at those which were predominantly black.

In 1965 the national education director of the NAACP was in Indianapolis to confer with the school board, and it was rumored that unless IPS adopted and implemented a policy against segregation it might be faced with litigation. The school board finally adopted a policy statement which directed the superintendent to make sure that employment practices were "fair." The statement reaffirmed belief in the "neighborhood school," while acknowledging that school districting could be used to promote desegregation. Spokesmen made clear that, while policy would be "flexible," there would be no busing.[4]

Adoption of the policy statement led to few changes. In 1967 the director of the Indiana Civil Rights Commission reported that most cities in Indiana, including Elkhart, Muncie, Evansville, Gary, and Anderson, had undertaken "positive" steps to end segregation but that Indianapolis was a glaring exception.

Early in 1968 a delegation from the Indianapolis branch of the NAACP met with the school board and presented a report which said that racial practices in IPS were "in violation of the spirit" of the 1954 desegregation decision of the Supreme Court and that failure to take steps to integrate school facilities was "an open and shut case of ignoring the laws of the land." Agents of the Department of Health, Education, and Welfare were reported to be observing the school system, and, most significantly, attorneys from the U.S. Department of Justice were in Indianapolis in response to a complaint by a parent.[5]

A few weeks later a letter from the assistant attorney general for civil rights accused the Indianapolis school system of "overt acts of racial discrimination in the assignment of students and faculty members." The action of the Justice Department was based on a section of the Civil Rights Act of 1964 which empowered the attorney general to act if he received a complaint in writing by a parent or group of parents to the effect that his or their minor children, as members of a class similarly situated, were being deprived by a school board of the equal protection of the laws. If the complaint was found to have merit and if taking action would "materially further the orderly achievement of segregation," and if the school authorities did not adjust the alleged conditions within a reasonable time, the Justice Department was authorized to institute a civil action in the district court in the name of the U.S. Government. The letter from the Justice Department listed a number of actions and policies alleged to be in violation of the 1964 law and said that there was a possibility of a suit if steps of compliance were not taken by May 6, 1968.[6]

An interval of sparring between the school board and the Justice Department lawyers followed. Not satisfied with the response of the IPS authorities, on May 31, 1968, the Justice Department filed an injunction against IPS in the United States District Court. Defendants were the Board of School Commissioners of the City of Indianapolis and the superintendent of schools.[7]

At this point it is perhaps appropriate to say something of the role of the Justice Department and Justice Department attorneys in the prolonged litigation. The suit, regarded as one of the first significant cases against a northern city under the 1964 act, began during the Johnson administration and dragged on through the Nixon-Ford years and into the Carter years. Changing attitudes and policies toward school desegregation and, in particular, toward remedies in the successive administrations were reflected in the positions of the attorneys in the Indianapolis case. Although the Justice Department began the litigation, on some occasions it sided with the defendants.

In wending our way through the intricacies of this prolonged litigation it will be helpful to keep in mind some chronology. The suit was begun in 1968; the district court did not hand down a decision until the summer of 1971. Ironically, in 1969, while the decision was pending, the state legislature enacted the law upon which the responsibility of the state of Indiana for perpetuating *de jure* racial segregation was ultimately to be decided—a key issue. I am referring to the law popularly known as the Uni-Gov Act, which was to distinguish the Indianapolis case from school desegregation cases in other northern cities, notably Detroit.

From the beginning the Uni-Gov proposal drew fire from the black community in Indianapolis, who saw it as motivated by the desire to weaken and dilute the influence of black voters. (It is probably not a coincidence that Uni-Gov was conceived after the election of Mayor Richard G. Hatcher in Gary.) The Uni-Gov act provided for the election of a mayor by voters of all of Marion County, including the incorporated cities of Speedway, Beech Grove, and Lawrence. A countywide council replaced the old city council. Certain services of Indianapolis and the surrounding townships were consolidated, but Uni-Gov did not create a unitary government. The act did not provide for metropolitan police and fire departments, nor, most important for our purposes, did it provide for a metropolitan school system.[8]

When the Justice Department filed the petition for an injunction against IPS in district court, members of the school board expressed complete surprise. The president of the board called the charge that they had not moved to comply with Justice Department requests "ridiculous." In answer to the charges (which we will discuss in more detail later), the school board made the following points: that there was "no hint of segregation in [the] assigning of pupils or teachers," that the neighborhood concept was sound and would remain board policy, that any one-race schools in Indianapolis were the result of "neighborhood characteristics," that the all-Negro character of Attucks "reflect[ed] the composition of the neighborhood surrounding the school," and that there was "nothing in the system to desegregate."[9]

In spite of these protests IPS did begin to take some limited steps toward increased desegregation. I cannot begin to go through all of the developments between the filing of the suit and the trial in the summer of 1971 but can give only a sampling. Even the most modest steps aroused opposition. When twenty-nine white teachers were appointed to the Attucks faculty, five of them resigned rather than accept the assignment.[10]

Headlines in the *Indianapolis Star* proclaimed: "CITIZEN'S GROUP WILL FIGHT U.S. MEDDLING IN SCHOOLS."[11]

The group, residents of the Northwest High School area styling themselves Citizens for Quality Schools, announced that they expected to get 20,000 to 40,000 signatures of persons opposed to the suit and that they would fight involuntary teacher assignments in the courts. School authorities who wanted to comply with Justice Department recommendations found themselves faced with a hostile public. A new superintendent (Stanley Campbell) was quoted as saying: "I won't hold up the neighborhood school concept as God's answer to education in the United States. It has its place, but I would not rely on it as a slogan or shibboleth about what to do about education in Indianapolis." He became an object of abuse and was dismissed.[12]

Early in 1970 IPS began to hold public hearings which were intended to give members of the community an opportunity to express their views about means of accomplishing desegregation. The first such meeting, at Arlington High School in January, when sub-zero temperatures were breaking records, attracted a crowd of about 1,500 for a debate which went on for four and one-half hours. About fifty-five persons spoke, two-thirds of them against any change in the neighborhood school concept. Pro-neighborhood speakers, with the exception of one who identified himself as spokesman for the United Klans of America, usually were careful to say that they believed in the equality of all persons without regard to race and favored racial integration but thought that it could come about gradually through residential integration and that any alteration in the neighborhood schools would lead to white flight from the city. Several threatened to boycott or defy any plan which violated the neighborhood concept. In reply, others pointed out that residential integration had not, in fact, occurred and was not likely to occur unless the schools themselves were first integrated. One representative of a neighborhood association said: "The decisions that will be made in the next few weeks regarding integration in the Indianapolis public schools are going to be unpopular decisions. It does not matter what these decisions might be—they are going to be unpopular."[13]

The truth of this prediction was abundantly confirmed in the following weeks and months as IPS struggled to come up with a plan that would satisfy the various elements of the Indianapolis community and would at the same time comply with some of the demands of lawyers of the Justice Department, with whom negotiations continued. Clearly the school board felt that it was most vulnerable legally on the question of Attucks High School. It had been created as a segregated school, and after 1949 the board had failed to redistrict so as to include white students in the enrollment, permitting instead the few white students who lived in the Attucks neighborhood to transfer to other high schools. In February, 1970, the board adopted a plan to phase out Attucks High School because it was all black and also to abolish Shortridge High School, where the percentage of blacks was so large that it threatened to become an all-black school. In place of the two schools a new Attucks would be built in a new location. However, the Justice Department found the proposal to build a new Attucks in a different location unacceptable because it meant that Attucks would continue as a segregated institution for at least three more years.[14]

On June 24, 1970, the Justice Department sent to Judge Dillin a bill of particulars of the charges which they expected to use against IPS at the anticipated trial. This document contained the essentials of the issues raised at the trial a year later. The Justice Department found the IPS system still largely segregated *de jure* twenty-one years after the state legislature had outlawed segregated schools and sixteen years after the Supreme Court's decision in *Brown v. Board of Education*.

The long awaited trial did not occur until August, 1971. In April of that year the United States Supreme Court handed down a decision in the case of *Swann* v. *Charlotte Mecklenberg Board of Education*.[15] This case deserves our attention because it furnished important guidelines for the decision in the Indianapolis case. A unanimous court, speaking through Chief Justice Warren Burger (a Nixon appointee), upheld busing as a legitimate remedy to effect the dismantling of a segregated school system. In the opinion, Burger, in an effort to provide guidance for justices in lower courts, pointed out a number of practices, such as the location of new schools and abandonment of old ones, drawing attendance zones, etc., which might be used to maintain a dual school system and thus perpetuate unlawful *de jure* segregation. He made a strong statement concerning the power of the judiciary under powers of equity to take whatever steps were necessary to remedy past wrongs.

At the trial, lawyers for the Justice Department presented an eighty-two page report, detailing the charges of *de jure* segregation by IPS, and urged the court to order certain measures which would result in the elimination of segregation "root and branch." On its side IPS denied the charges, insisting that the existence of all-black, or predominantly black, or all-white, or predominantly white, schools was not due to any practice or policy of the school board— that present racial characteristics of the city schools were due entirely to residential patterns.[16]

Judge Dillin handed down a lengthy decision August 18, 1971.[17] It should be considered in two parts. First, IPS was found guilty of *de jure* segregation, "operating a segregated school system wherein segregation was imposed by law." In reaching the decision the judge presented massive amounts of evidence, including a summary of the history of race relations and segregation in Indiana. He found that after the state law of 1949, intended to eliminate segregation, and after the Supreme Court decision in *Brown* v. *Board of Education* in 1954, the Indianapolis school board continued policies which perpetuated and actually increased segregation. Specifically he cited zoning policies (i.e., drawing of school districts). According to evidence presented at the trial, there had been 360 boundary changes since 1954, of which more than 90 percent promoted segregation. In addition, optional attendance zones in areas with racially mixed populations gave students a choice between attending predominantly white or predominantly black schools. "Feeder" elementary school districts were drawn so as to prevent assignment of white students to Attucks. A "Save Shortridge" plan which had been adopted to prevent Shortridge from becoming all black had arranged feeder districts to insure that Attucks would remain all black. During the 1950s and 1960s, a period when the increases in the number of persons of school age necessitated building new schools and enlarging old ones, additions were built to existing old Negro schools instead of transferring black pupils from overcrowded black schools to white schools with vacant classrooms.[18] Sites for new high schools were chosen on the edges of Indianapolis so as to minimize the number of black enrollees. The court enjoined IPS from discriminating on the basis of race in the operation of the Indianapolis school system, ordering that the following steps be taken to implement the decision: (1) immediate assignment of faculty and staff to insure "that no school is racially identifiable from the composition of faculty or staff," (2) immediate continuation of plans to desegregate and relocate Attucks, (3) revision of transfer policies, and (4) negotiation with outside school corporations for possible transfer of minority students.[19]

Dillin recognized that these steps would not result in significant desegregation of schools with black majorities. In the second and more innovative part of his decision he sought to find a lasting solution to the "tipping point" issue and the possible involvement of outlying school corporations and the state of Indiana in the suit. The court pointed out that there was undisputed evidence that when the number of black students in a given school approached 40 percent of the total, exodus of whites was hastened and became irreversible. This quickly resulted in resegregation in cities which had undertaken desegregation plans, the central city becoming virtually an all-Negro city within a city. The example of Atlanta was cited as the "brutal truth" of what happened when a city undertook in good faith "to apply across the board desegregation" in a situation where racial balances had reached the "tipping point." In a ten-year period in Atlanta the school population had changed from 70 percent white and 30 percent Negro to 70 percent Negro and 30 percent white. Other cities which had undertaken desegregation with what the court called "tunnel vision" had had similar experiences.

"It is obvious," the court continued, "that something more than a routine, computerized approach to the problem of desegregation is required . . . lest the tipping point be reached and passed beyond retrieve." It added: "The easy way out for this Court and for the Board would be to order a massive 'fruit basket' scrambling of students within the School City during the coming year, to achieve exact racial balancing and then to go on to other things. The pressure to do so is undoubted. There is just one thing wrong with this simplistic solution, in the long haul it won't work." An Indianapolis only plan could furnish no lasting solution, but: "Realistically, it is clear that the tipping point resegregation would pale into insignificance if the Board's jurisdiction were coterminous with that of Uni-Gov," and would be minimized still further if certain school systems in adjoining counties which were part of the Indianapolis metropolitan area were included.[20]

The Uni-Gov law, while consolidating some departments of government, expressly provided that school corporations were not affected. "Thus," said the court, "Uni-Gov leaves the defendant School City exactly where it found it, confined to an area in the central part of the consolidated city of Indianapolis, where it is surrounded by eight township school systems operating independently within the purportedly unified city, and by the two additional independent school corporations operated by Beech Grove and Speedway." In this outlying school system during 1969–1970, blacks made up only 2.62 percent of the total enrollment, while out of more than three thousand teachers only fifteen were black—less than one-half of one percent.

Under Supreme Court rulings, "All provisions of federal, state or local law requiring or permitting racial discrimination in public education must yield to the principle that such discrimination is unconstitutional." This standard raised the question of whether the General Assembly should provide for the creation of a metropolitan school district in order "to purge the state of its role in contributing to *de jure* segregation in the Indianapolis School System." This and other questions concerning responsibility of state agencies for segregation led the court to order that the state of Indiana be made a defendant in the case and that township school corporations in Marion County and certain school corporations in surrounding counties be added as defendants.[21]

To summarize: Judge Dillin found IPS guilty of perpetuating unconstitutional *de jure* segregation and ordered certain steps to remedy the situation, but discovered that no lasting answer could be found within the boundaries of the old city and therefore ordered that the Justice Department add the township school corporations as defendants as well as the state of Indiana to determine its responsibility for perpetuating segregation.

By a margin of four to three the school board voted to appeal the decision, and a few days after the school board filed its appeal John Moss, a local black attorney, filed a motion to intervene in the case by added plaintiffs. The motion on behalf of Donny Brurell Buckley and Alycia Marquese Buckley, as representatives of a class composed of Negro children of school age in Marion County, asked the court to require the defendants to submit a plan which conformed to the Equal Protection Clause of the Fourteenth Amendment and sought to have parts of the Uni-Gov act declared unconstitutional. Henceforth Moss and his associate John Preston Ward played a more active and aggressive role in the litigation than the lawyers for the Justice Department.[22]

The Seventh Circuit Court of Appeals upheld the district court's decision that IPS was guilty of *de jure* segregation in February, 1973, saying that years of deliberate segregation prior to 1949 had obligated the school board to take affirmative action "to eliminate all vestiges of segregation 'root and branch,'" but that it had failed to do so. The appeals court agreed with the lower court in finding "a purposeful pattern of racial discrimination based on the aggregate of many decisions of the board and its agents." In June, 1973, the United States Supreme Court denied an appeal by the Indianapolis school board for a review.[23]

While holding IPS guilty, the appeals court sent back to the district court the question of determining the responsibility of the state of Indiana and the issue of whether the suburban school corporations should be included in the remedy for segregation in the Indianapolis schools.

Although the Justice Department had brought the original suit against IPS, at the trial in 1973 it did not urge a metropolitan plan, which would have involved large-scale busing (which was opposed by the Nixon administration), but submitted a plan for an Indianapolis only plan, insisting that it would be workable.

John Moss, the attorney who had entered the case in behalf of the black children, asked that a unified school plan for central Indiana be adopted and argued: "Uni-Gov, to the extent that it leaves out the schools, is legislative gerrymandering. It binds minority pupils into a certain section of Indianapolis and denies them equal educational opportunities." A brief filed by lawyers for the Coalition for Integrated Education, a group which had been given amicus standing, emphasized the responsibility of the state for schools under the Indiana constitution and argued that if the General Assembly and state authorities failed to act to desegregate, "or if they act in a manner inconsistent with the expeditious and efficient elimination of unconstitutional practices . . . the court has the authority to invoke its equitable powers to fashion such a remedy."[24]

Much of the trial was consumed with the question of the responsibility of the state of Indiana for the perpetuation of segregation and its responsibility for a remedy. The issue was whether any of the state officials "had acted to promote segregation, or failed to carry out duties imposed on them by law in such a manner as to promote segregation or inhibit desegregation in IPS," and "whether or not the acts of *de jure* segregation hitherto found to have been practiced by IPS can be imputed to the State of Indiana such that appropriate State officials or agencies may be directed to afford relief to vindicate the Fourteenth Amendment rights of plaintiffs and their class."[25]

In response to these questions the attorneys for the state emphasized the control of schools by local corporations and denied that the state or its agents were in any way responsible for actions or policies which perpetuated segregation. The opinion of the court presented voluminous evidence to refute this position, citing an impressive array of Indiana Supreme Court opinions showing the responsibility of the state over local school administration. Judge Dillin emphasized the power of the state under Article 8 of the Indiana Constitution, which gave almost unlimited power to the General Assembly to regulate the school system. In carrying out its educational functions the state might use local corporations, but these corporations were agents of the state for the purpose of administering the state system of education. In addition to citing court cases, the judge pointed out that the *Indiana Code* of 1971 included 349 solid pages, single spaced in small type, of statutes enacted by the General Assembly "regulating virtually every phase of school operations." The annotated version of these laws filled two volumes and comprised 1,154 pages.[26]

Of special importance in the present case was a statute which vested in the Indiana State Board of Education, through a director appointed by the state superintendent, the power and duty to regulate new school sites and buildings and also additions to existing buildings. Most damaging to the state was the evidence concerning the sites for three new Indianapolis high schools (Arlington, Northwest, and John Marshall), all located on the extreme outer limits of IPS and all opening with virtually no black enrollment. Sites for the schools had been approved by agents of the State Board of Education and the Superintendent of Public Instruction. The court found: "The officials of State charged with oversight of the common schools have done almost literally nothing, and certainly next to nothing, to furnish leadership, guidance, and direction in this critical area." Instead it concluded: "The Court finds that the failure of the State Superintendent and the Board of Education to act affirmatively in support of the law was an omission tending to inhibit desegregation."[27]

On the question of the added defendant school corporations (the suburban school systems), the court admitted that there was no evidence that any of them had committed *de jure* segregation because, as the judge remarked ironically, none of them had had an opportunity to commit such overt acts since the black population in their school districts ranged from "slight to none." In considering why there was such a "remarkable absence of Negro citizens" in all the suburban school districts, the court heard expert testimony which showed that racial discrimination in housing in the suburbs was "a root cause of the black central city phenomenon." The court concluded that since the present case was not an action having to do with discrimination in housing, it was not appropriate to try to remedy that discrimination in a school discrimination suit, but that there was an obvious relationship between housing and the absence of blacks in the schools.[28]

The judge concluded that a lasting remedy to segregation in IPS was impossible without including the suburban schools. He declared that the General Assembly had the power and duty to devise a plan for metropolitan desegregation. Since the state had been guilty of the discrimination which led to segregation it certainly had the power to remedy it by crossing boundary lines of school corporations if necessary. However, if the state legislature failed to act within a reasonable time, he asserted that the court had the power to devise its own plan.[29]

As a measure of interim relief the judge ordered the suburban school corporations in Marion County to accept a reasonable number of Negro children from IPS on a transfer basis at the beginning of the 1973–74 school year, the cost of transportation and tuition to be paid by IPS.[30]

Although litigation dragged on for another eight years, in the long run the essential features of Judge Dillin's decision in the summer of 1973 were upheld. The nub of this decision, and the thing that made it significant, was that a lasting remedy for *de jure* segregation was impossible within the boundaries of IPS and that what Dillin called the "artificial" barriers of suburban school corporations must be crossed to achieve a long-range solution to the problem of segregation in IPS.

As I have said, litigation—appeals, stays of court orders, etc.— dragged on for years longer, and since I am not embarking upon an entire semester's course, but am giving a single lecture, I shall try to summarize later developments.

First of all—the immediate community reaction. Dillin's decision calling for transportation of black pupils to the suburbs brought cries of protest from the public, while the state of Indiana expressed outrage at being held responsible for perpetuating segregation.

A reactivated Citizens Against Busing Group began circulating petitions for a constitutional amendment to prevent assignment of pupils on the basis of race, while urging the members of the General Assembly not to take action on Dillin's instructions to them. Not content with this, the leaders of the group, a former state senator and a Marion County circuit judge, began a campaign to impeach Judge Dillin, denouncing his decision as "unconstitutional, unlawful, and dictatorial."[31]

In reply to his critics, Judge Dillin attempted to instruct them and the public in a few principles of constitutional law and the function of federal judges. Of members of the school board who had run on an anti-busing platform, he had earlier said:

> You can run on any platform you want to run on, but friends, you will have to understand that if things you espouse in your platform turn out to be constitutionally impermissible, then you cannot legally implement your platform.

Even assuming the neighborhood school can adequately be defined in law—which I doubt—to the extent that it might conflict with a constitutional duty to desegregate a school system which has been de jure segregated, then that policy must yield.

In reply to the advocates of impeachment he issued a statement which said: "It is the undoubted right of every citizen to express his opinion as to the wisdom of any rule of law, and to work for changes if he feels sufficiently strongly on the subject. However the law cannot be changed in any trial court, such as the Federal court in Indianapolis." The purpose of the statement, he said, was to "demonstrate why your court and all judges who take seriously their oaths of office are required to follow the law, even if public opinion appears at the time to be adverse to the law itself, or to its enforcement."[32]

In spite of the cries of outrage at Dillin's decision by the politicians, the Indiana General Assembly took steps to comply with his instructions to them. Before the meeting of the 1974 session of the legislature, the judge gave them broad options as to legislation which would fulfill their obligations regarding desegregation. Quoting at length from the opinion of the Supreme Court in the Swann case concerning the powers of federal judges, he reminded them that if they did not take action he would do so.[33] The legislature responded with a lengthy act dealing with court ordered transfers of students from one corporation to another, providing formulas for paying the costs of transportation and tuition and distribution of state funds.[34]

The state of Indiana and the lawyers for the suburban school corporations pinned their hopes for a reversal of Dillin on the decision in the Detroit school desegregation case pending in the Supreme Court. Amicus briefs were filed by counsel for Lawrence, Warren, and Wayne townships and by the state attorney general.

In the case of *Milliken* v. *Bradley* a bitterly divided Supreme Court (by a five-to-four decision) overruled a lower court decision, rejecting the argument that the state of Michigan and local officials by reason of official policies were responsible for segregation in the Detroit school system. A metropolitan area-wide desegregation plan which included suburban school districts was rejected.[35]

In Indiana great elation among state officials and lawyers for the suburban schools followed the decision, but rejoicing proved premature. In August, 1974, after the Detroit decision, the Seventh Circuit Court of Appeals upheld Judge Dillin on the question of the responsibility of the state of Indiana, declaring that "state officials, by various acts and omissions, promoted segregation and inhibited desegregation within IPS." The appeals court declared that the state had an affirmative duty to assist the IPS board in desegregating within its boundaries. The appeals court, at this time, did not uphold the inclusion of outlying suburban school corporations in a desegregation plan, nor did it rule out that possibility. Instead, it raised the crucial question of whether the adoption of the Uni-Gov law by the General Assembly was an attempt to perpetuate segregation. It ordered Dillin "to determine whether the establishment of Uni-Gov boundaries . . . warrants an interdistrict remedy within Uni-Gov."[36]

In an opinion issued in August, 1975, Judge Dillin, after reviewing evidence at the time of the adoption of Uni-Gov in 1969 declared: "When the General Assembly (which under state and federal law had a duty to alleviate segregation in IPS) expressly eliminated the school system from consideration under Uni-Gov, it signaled its lack of concern with the whole problem and inhibited desegregation." As further evidence he cited the fact that suburban townships had resisted earlier plans for school consolidation and ceased resisting Uni-Gov only when it was made clear that schools would not be included. He based his authority to order one-way busing to the suburban schools on the failure to include schools in the Uni-Gov consolidation.[37]

In December, 1975, the Court of Appeals heard arguments on the question of busing to suburban schools and on Uni-Gov in particular. Lawyers for the intervening defendants (the black children) sought to show that the history of racial policies in Indiana made the Indianapolis case different from the Detroit case. One of the judges asked one of the lawyers for the defense, who argued that the position of the state of Indiana on segregation had been merely one of "benign neglect," "Do you think in reality, that the opposition to the consolidation of the schools was not really a racially motivated opposition? In other words, if Marion County were all white or all black, would there still be opposition to [school] consolidation?"[38]

The following July the Court of Appeals in a lengthy opinion, which distinguished the Indianapolis case from the Detroit case, upheld the district court. In his opinion Justice Luther Swygert quoted at length the majority opinion of Chief Justice Burger in that case. Although in that case the court had ruled against interdistrict busing as a remedy, Burger's opinion suggested that under some circumstances it would be acceptable. He said before school districts could be changed, before an interdistrict remedy could be imposed, there must be evidence of "a constitutional violation within the district that produces a significant segregative effect on another district. *Specifically, it must be shown that racially discriminatory acts of the state or local school districts, or of a single school district have been a substantial cause of interdistrict segregation.*" In the Indianapolis case Swygert found evidence of "significant segregative effect" in two laws—Uni-Gov and another law I have not mentioned which passed almost unnoticed sixteen days before the adoption of Uni-Gov, at a time when members of the legislature knew that the school suit was pending in the district court. This act had repealed a 1961 act which provided that school boundaries would automatically be extended when civil boundaries were extended. This "fail safe" measure, said the judge, showed that the legislature intended to make sure that the boundaries of IPS would not expand with those of the civil city. Having thus guaranteed that there would be no school consolidation, the legislature passed the Uni-Gov law. "In summary," said the court, "we are convinced that the essential findings for an interdistrict remedy found lacking [in Detroit] are supplied by the record in the instant [Indianapolis] case." In Detroit, he pointed out, school boundaries and city boundaries were coterminous and had been established more than a century earlier.[39]

Thus the responsibility of the state of Indiana for perpetuating *de jure* segregation and the question of interdistrict busing as a remedy appeared to be settled, but what about the original defendant, IPS, which had been ordered to desegregate within its own borders and to bus some of its black students to the suburbs? Here it is necessary for me to summarize as briefly as possible. After the 1973 decision of the district court, the Indianapolis Board of School Commissioners, evidently convinced that the city schools at least must be desegregated, began to take grudging steps toward compliance. However, because the board failed to come up with a plan for desegregation which the judge considered adequate, he appointed two commissioners who drew up a pupil assignment plan which was an attempt to conform to guidelines in Burger's opinion in the Swann case. Some busing for purposes of desegregation began in Indianapolis in 1973, years before the issue of interdistrict busing was settled.

Dillin's 1973 decision for one-way busing to the suburbs raised two new issues for IPS—the effect on school enrollments and hence on teachers' jobs and the question of the fairness of one-way busing as a remedy. In anticipation of the probable effect of transfer of large numbers of black students to the suburbs early in 1974, the superintendent of IPS sent letters to hundreds of tenured teachers informing them that their contracts would not be renewed because of the probable elimination of their jobs. However, because of delays in implementation of the transfers to the suburbs the teachers were rehired.[40]

Before the final steps in the prolonged litigation, important changes occurred in the Indianapolis Board of School Commissioners itself. In 1976 the Citizens School Committee, a self-perpetuating body which had selected candidates and dominated school board elections for more than forty years, was in disarray and lost control. The seven members elected in 1976 were candidates of a group calling itself CHOICE (Citizens Helping Out Indianapolis Children's Education). Their election signaled a change in position in the litigation and on the question of busing. The new group asked for a rehearing of the school case on two grounds—that one-way busing was discriminatory to black students, and that it would lead to dismissal of a substantial number of IPS teachers and place an undue financial burden on IPS. They asked the appeals court to grant a stay to Dillin's order for busing black students to the suburbs on the grounds that it "cast the entire burden of desegregation on those whose rights were violated." They announced that they intended to present a plan for two-way busing and asked that the district court be ordered to hold a remedy hearing. Instead of one-way busing they proposed two alternatives: two-way busing bringing white suburban pupils into Indianapolis, or a unitary school system for all of Marion County, the plan which they preferred. Moreover, the new school board sought to change its position from that of defendant to plaintiff. Judge Dillin agreed to allow the board to present alternatives to plans for one-way busing, but he rejected their request to change position from defendant to plaintiff, which they asked because they did not hold the same views on busing as their predecessors on the board.[41] The judge said he could not allow the change merely because it was due to the outcome of the 1976 election, declaring: "The next election may well reverse the board's position once again. This court should not be required to realign the parties following each election." He again reaffirmed his plan for one-way busing to the suburbs, reiterating the reason for rejecting two-way busing which he had stated earlier: that the "court had no power to order that a suburban child be transferred out of its own school corporation so long as the suburban school corporations remain separate legal entities." In his order he said that teachers of IPS who were displaced by the one-way busing plan should be part of a pool from which the suburban schools would draw to fill needs created by the transfer of pupils from the city system.[42]

In a final opinion in the case in April, 1980, the court of appeals affirmed one-way busing as the remedy, noting that within the boundaries of the old city of Indianapolis white children as well as black would be reassigned and bused. In October, 1980, the United States Supreme Court again refused to grant a review of the Indianapolis case as it had consistently done on previous appeals. Headlines in the *Indianapolis Star* asked: "ONE WAY BUSING THIS JANUARY?" The headlines did not suggest that the highest court, the final authority in the land, had upheld the decision of the district court by refusing to review.[43]

Buses to the suburban school actually did not begin to roll until the beginning of the 1981–82 school year. And as the fateful date approached, the tone of the headlines changed. "POLL SHOWS RESIDENTS EXPECT SCHOOL BUSING TO BE PEACE-FUL," said one. A group of civic leaders organized an advisory council entitled PRIDE (Peaceful Response to Indianapolis Desegregation Education). The mayor of Indianapolis proclaimed the weekend before the opening of school, "School Desegregation with Pride Weekend." With rare exceptions everything was orderly as suburban schools opened their doors to the black enrollees.[44]

But there remained some unresolved legal questions. As it had become increasingly evident that busing was actually going to take place, the question of who was going to pay the monetary costs became more urgent. A number of bills intended to block payment in case the state was ordered to pay the costs were introduced into the General Assembly, none of which passed both houses. The district court ruled that the state of Indiana, having been found responsible for perpetuating unlawful segregation, should pay transportation and tuition costs of students bused to the suburbs. After the district court was upheld by the appeals court and the Supreme Court, the governor said grudgingly that the state would abide by the ruling.[45]

And so the threats of defiance sputtered and died, and the state and the public began to live with the reality of interdistrict busing as a remedy for past discrimination and segregation. The constitutional issues were settled, but human relations problems of students transported to a new environment were just beginning.

This brings us to the question which I have largely ignored because of limitations of time and because it is not a strictly legal question—the response of the black community to one-way busing as the remedy for past injuries—a remedy which many found it difficult to accept. From the day of the district court decision in 1973 some blacks expressed resentment at what they regarded as a discriminatory remedy—one which, in the words of one civic leader, made black children "sacrificial lambs," placing upon them an unfair burden for a wrong for which they were not responsible. Blacks were concerned that children transported to suburban schools would not be able to participate fully in extracurricular activities and social affairs, while parents were concerned that they would not be able to share in determining school policies. These fears led to the latest legal development in this prolonged litigation. (I will not be so brash as to predict that it will be the final one.) Black parents, seeking a solution to some of the problems I have mentioned, filed a suit in federal district court as an addition to the original desegregation suit, claiming that denying them the vote in township school elections was a violation of Fourteenth Amendment rights. In response, Judge Dillin issued an order granting parents the right to vote in school elections in the townships to which their children were bused. This decision enabled them to vote in the school board elections of May, 1984.[46]

Just a few concluding observations. The Indianapolis School Busing Case is unique. The thing that makes it unique—that distinguishes it from desegregation cases in other cities—is the Uni-Gov Act by which the state legislature carefully excluded schools from the metropolitan government. By doing so the legislature was found by the courts to have had racially discriminatory intent, which made possible an interdistrict remedy (i.e., busing to the suburbs) for segregation in the Indianapolis schools.

But I think the larger significance of the case is the recognition by the district court of the futility of an Indianapolis only plan for desegregation—the court's determination to find a remedy which would not lead to resegregation. The necessity for such a remedy is summed up in a comment by Judge Dillin in the 1973 decision when, after having determined the responsibility of the state of Indiana for perpetuating segregation, he said: "There exists, however, an even more compelling basis for this court's crossing artificial boundary lines to cure the State's constitutional violation. If we hold that school district boundaries are absolute barriers to an IPS desegregation plan, we would be opening a way to nullify *Brown* v. *Board of Education*." This was really the heart of the matter.

Under Judge Dillin's plan the largely all-white suburban school districts shared with the central city in the desegregation process and assignment of pupils. Although there was two-way busing within the boundaries of IPS, the number of pupils transported was smaller than would have been the case in an Indianapolis only plan. By fashioning a remedy which reduced the probability of resegregation, perhaps Judge Dillin also reduced social tensions and hostilities which have accompanied desegregation in some cities.

Notes

1. Emma Lou Thornbrough, *Since Emancipation, A Short History of Indiana Negroes 1863–1963* (Indianapolis: Indiana Division American Negro Emancipation Centennial Authority, 1963), 55–56.

2. Ibid., 51–61.

3. 374 U.S. 483 (1954). The Equal Protection Clause of the Fourteenth Amendment: "No State shall . . . deny to any person within its jurisdiction the equal protection of the laws."

4. *Indianapolis News*, April 30, 1965; *Indianapolis Star*, January 7, 1968.

5. *Indianapolis News*, February 28, 1968; *Indianapolis Star*, February 28, 1968.

6. 42 U.S.C. & 2000 - 6(a) and (b).

7. *U.S. v. Board of School Commissioners, Indianapolis, Indiana*, 332 F Supp 655.

8. An Act concerning reorganization or government in counties containing a city of the first class, *Laws of the State of Indiana Passed at the Ninety-Sixth Regular Session of the General Assembly* (1969), 357–448; *Indianapolis Recorder*, March 1, 1969.

9. *Indianapolis News*, June 20, 1968.

10. *Indianapolis Star*, December 28, 29, 1968.

11. Ibid., November 22, 1968. Headlines in the major Indianapolis newspapers usually emphasized the more sensational aspects of the desegregation case, but the articles in both the *Star* and the *News* gave accurate and quite thorough coverage.

12. *Indianapolis News*, August 27, 1969; *Indianapolis Star*, July 18, 1972.

13. *Indianapolis News*, January 21, 1970.

14. Ibid., February 3, March 30, 1970; January 2, 1971.

15. 402 U.S. 1 (1971).

16. *Indianapolis News*, August 6, 1971.

17. *United States v. Board of School Commissioners, Indianapolis, Indiana*, 332 D Supp 655.

18. Ibid., 656–60.

19. Ibid., 680. Under Dillin's order only about 1 percent of pupils in Indianapolis would be bused, a much smaller number than recommended by the Justice Department.

20. Ibid., 678.

21. Ibid., 679–80.

22. *Indianapolis News*, September 1, 10, October 22, 1971.

23. Ibid., June 25, 1973; 474 F 2d 81; 413 U.S. 920.

24. *Indianapolis Star*, June 11, 1973; *Indianapolis News*, June 6, 12, 26, July 12, 1973.

25. *United States of America, Plaintiff, Donny Brurell Buckley, Alycia Marquese Buckley, by their parent and next friend, Ruby L. Buckley, on behalf of themselves and all Negro school children residing in the area served by original defendants herein, Intervening Plaintiffs v. The Board of School Commissioners of the City of Indianapolis, Indiana, et al. Defendants Otis R. Bowen as Governor of the State of Indiana et al. Added Defendants, Citizens for Quality Schools, Inc., Intervening Defendant, Coalition for Integrated Education, Amicus Curiae. Hamilton Southeastern School, Hamilton County, Indiana, et al. Additional Added Defendants*. 468 F Supp 1191, 1197.

26. Ibid., 1200–1203.

27. Ibid., 1203.

28. Ibid., 1205.

29. Ibid.

30. Ibid., 1208.

31. *Indianapolis News*, July 23, 1973; *Indianapolis Star*, August 25, 1973.

32. *Indianapolis News*, July 9, 1973; *Indianapolis Star*, August 31, 1973.

33. *Indianapolis News*, December 7, 1973.

34. Public Law No. 94, *Laws of the State of Indiana Passed at Second Regular Session of the Ninety-eighth General Assembly* (1974), 345. The law applied "solely in a situation where a court of the United States or the State of Indiana" found a school corporation "has violated the equal protection clause of the Fourteenth Amendment to the Constitution of the United States by practicing de jure segregation of the students within its borders."

35. *Indianapolis Star*, December 30, 1973; *Milliken v. Bradley*, 418 U.S. 717 (1974).

36. 503 F 2d 68. At this time the appeals court rejected the inclusion of thirteen non-Marion County school corporations as added defendants. Meanwhile, on July 3, 1974, Judge Dillin had ordered IPS to continue existing school assignments through 1974–75 pending a final decision by the appeals court on a metropolitan plan.

37. 419 F Supp 183. In this opinion Judge Dillin also cited public housing as evidence of segregationist policy, pointing out that 98 percent of residents of public housing, all located within the old city boundaries, were black, and that their children attended IPS schools. At this time he prohibited the renovation of Lockfield Gardens, built during the 1930s as public housing for blacks, as family type housing and ordered the Indianapolis Housing Authority not to build any additional family type public housing within IPS boundaries.

38. *Indianapolis News*, December 4, 1975.

39. 541 F 2d 1211. In affirming the decision of the district court the appeals court suggested that the lower court monitor the transfer of black pupils from IPS to other school districts periodically. There was one more complication over Uni-Gov before the final implementation of Dillin's order for the beginning of busing to the suburbs. The Supreme Court, with three justices dissenting, remanded the case to the Seventh Circuit Court of Appeals, with instructions to give it further consideration in the light of two recent decisions, *Village of Arlington Heights v. Metropolitan Housing Corporation* and *Washington v. Davis*. In both of these cases the Supreme Court had injected the issue of whether actions which resulted in

perpetuating segregation had been racially motivated. The court of appeals now remanded the case to the district court with instructions to determine "whether relevant acts or omissions of state and local officials were motivated, at least in part, by racially discriminatory purpose or intent as articulated in Washington v. Davis and Arlington Heights."

On remand the district court found that exclusion of schools from the Uni-Gov legislation "was done with a racially discriminatory purpose." It also found discriminatory purpose in the failure of the Housing Authority of Indianapolis to build any units outside the old central city. At the same time Dillin held that the law passed by the legislature in 1974 allowed him to implement the interdistrict remedy without regard to the question of legislative intent posed by the Supreme Court. The court of appeals then again reaffirmed the plan for interdistrict busing, deciding that the conclusion of "discriminatory purpose" in repeal of the 1961 school law was justified. It also affirmed the district court on the question of Public Housing, 329 U.S. 1068; 573 F 2d 400; 637 F 2d 1101.

40. *Indianapolis News*, April 19, 22, 1974. The Indiana State Teachers Association, which asked to be allowed to intervene in the school suit to protect jobs and have a voice in the educational aspects of any plan which the district court devised, became a party in the later stages of litigation.

41. *Indianapolis Star*, July 2, 1978; *Indianapolis News*, August 12, 1978; *Indianapolis Star*, September 21, 1978. The school board also hired two nationally known civil rights lawyers to assist them in the case, but Judge Dillin refused to allow them to represent IPS because both had appeared earlier in the case on the side of the black plaintiffs and against the Board of School Commissioners.

42. 506 F Supp 657; *Indianapolis Star*, September 21, 1978.

43. 637 F 2d 1107; 449 U.S. 838; *Indianapolis Star*, October 7, 1980.

44. *Indianapolis Star*, June 13, August 15, 1981.

45. Ibid., December 14, 1982.

46. *Indianapolis News*, July 21, 1973, August 10, 1975, January 7, 1983; *Indianapolis Star*, January 24, 1983, March 10, 16, 1984.

47. 368 F Supp 1205.

Bible Biology:
Hendren v.
Indiana Textbook Commission

Irving L. Fink

Mr. Fink is associated with the law firm of Townsend Yosha Cline & Price and served as counsel in Hendren *v.* Indiana Textbook Commission.

The Indiana State Commission on Textbook Adoption on December 12, 1975, selected as one of the seven textbooks approved for biology classes, grades nine to twelve, the book entitled *Biology: A Search for Order in Complexity*. The book was prepared by the Textbook Committee of the Creation Research Society and published by Zondervan Publishing House. It was edited by John N. Moore and Harold Schultz Slusher. The adoption by the commission was made pursuant to I.C. 20–10.1–9–1 et seq. The adoption period of the book was to run from July 1, 1976, through June 20, 1981. The State Superintendent of Public Instruction, Dr. Harold H. Negley, as chairman of the textbook commission, notified school executives throughout the state of the textbook adoption. Thereafter, textbook selection from the approved lists took place by the local governing bodies for the respective jurisdictions.

Prior to July 1, 1976, and pursuant to I.C. 20–10.1–9–22, seven local school systems notified the commission that they had adopted the biology textbook in question for their schools. Those schools were West Clark Community Schools, South Ripley Community School Corporation, Bango Community Schools, Union Township Schools, Warsaw Community Schools, East Washington School Corporation, and MSD Martinsville. The first two school systems above selected the book as their sole textbook for biology classes. The others selected the book along with at least one other textbook.

Early in July, 1976, the Indiana Civil Liberties Union was contacted by some parents of children in the West Clark Community Schools. They were distressed by the selection of the biology textbook for their school and felt that the use of the book might constitute an illegal abridgement of constitutional separation of church and state.

* * * *

There is no subject in our private life, perhaps, which can be more divisive or can give rise to more passion than that of religion and the state, particularly as it involves children in the public schools. We should recall the background of the founders of this nation and the framers of our Constitution. They wanted to keep religion out of politics and harbored special fears of the government interjecting itself into matters of religion, whether by limiting the freedom of people worshiping as they pleased or in establishing a state religion.

The First Amendment, which was adopted in December, 1791, stated in part:

> Congress shall make no law respecting an establishment of religion, or prohibiting the free exercise thereof.

The Supreme Court of the United States in a number of cases dealing with the Establishment Clause of the First Amendment has referred to "the wall of separation between church and state." See *Reynolds* v. *United States*, 98 U.S. 145, 164 (1878); *Everson* v. *Board of Education*, 330 U.S. 1, 18 (1947). The phrase undoubtedly came from a reply of President Thomas Jefferson to an address by a committee of the Danbury Baptist Association, January 1, 1802, when he wrote:

> I contemplate with sovereign reverence that act of the whole American people which declared that their legislature should "make no law respecting an establishment of religion, or prohibiting the free exercise thereof," thus building a wall of separation between church and state (R. Freeman Butz, *The American Tradition in Religion and Education* [Beacon Press, 1950], p. 92).

While the concept of a "wall of separation" might be a useful figure of speech in applying constitutional principles arising out of the First Amendment, it must be recognized that no real wall has existed for a lengthy period of time. In *Lynch* v. *Donnelly*, 45 U.S. 668, 670 (1984), the decision involving the creche erected by the town of Pawtucket, Rhode Island, the Supreme Court pointed out:

> It is clear that neither the seventeen draftsmen of the Constitution who were members of the First Congress, nor the Congress of 1789, saw any establishment problem in the employment of congressional Chaplains to offer daily prayers in the Congress, a practice that has continued for nearly two centuries. It would be difficult to identify a more striking example of the accommodation of religious belief intended by the Framers.

Other holes in the wall of separation are those involving the phrases "In God We Trust" on our currency and "One Nation Under

God," which was added as a part of the Pledge of Allegiance to the American flag.

Nonetheless, the Supreme Court has been traditionally strong in asserting the separation of church and state when it comes to injecting religion in the public schools. The case of *Engel* v. *Vitale*, 370 U.S. 421 (1962), struck down as unconstitutional the reading of a state-composed prayer in the public schools of New York. In *Abington School District* v. *Schempp*, 374 U.S. 203 (1963), the Court held that the schools could not require or permit students to read publicly passages from the Bible at the beginning of the school day.

The Fourteenth Amendment, Section One reads:

> All persons born or naturalized in the United States and subject to the jurisdiction thereof are citizens of the United States and of the State wherein they reside. No state shall make or enforce any law which shall abridge the privileges or immunities of citizens of the United States; nor shall any State deprive any person of life, liberty, or property without due process of law; nor deny to any person within its jurisdiction the equal protection of the laws.

The Fourteenth Amendment became law in 1868. Not until 1940, however, did the Supreme Court specifically rule that the clauses pertaining to religion in the First Amendment were likewise applicable to the states under the due process clause of the Fourteenth Amendment. See *Cantwell* v. *Connecticut*, 310 U.S. 296 (1940).

*   *   *   *

Some of the individuals on the Indiana Civil Liberties Union Screening Committee began an investigation and evaluation of the biology textbook which had been brought to their attention, as well as the Teacher's Guide for use of the book and certain brochures advertising the book. A brochure of Creation Life Publishers, a group which apparently had nothing to do with developing the book but which helped take over the distribution for Zondervan Publishing House, stated:

> We are seeking to inform the public about the latest findings regarding special creation, but we also desire and publish and distribute to put material which will educate the reader concerning scripture role evidences and religious thought and which will build up the body of

Christ. For these reasons and others, we have entered into the publication and distribution of specific textbooks for both Christian and public schools. We expect to expand our publishing in this area of great need. We are a very personal company, committed to a mission of publishing and educating to make all God's word and well known [sic].

Dr. Henry M. Morris, a former president of Creation Research Society, the developers of the textbook, stated in a published letter:

> I would strongly advise parents to send their own children to Christian schools if at all possible even while they continue to do all they can to restore sound morality in education practices through the public schools of their communities.

Most significantly the preface stated that the most reasonable explanation for the actual facts of biology as they are known scientifically is that of biblical creationism. It went on to say:

> We hope this approach will be attractive first of all to the many private schools directed by those seeking to maintain an educational philosophy and methodology consistent with traditional Christian perspectives. We trust it will also be of interest and use in public school systems by teachers desiring to develop a genuine scientific attitude in their students, rather than an artificially induced evolutionary worldview. (xxiii)

The textbook itself contained such passages as the following:

> A primary purpose of science should be to learn about God's handywork. (p. 13)

> The scientist does not deal with God as a subject of science; he deals rather with the laws and principles God has established. (p. 7)

> The marvelous mountains are a proof of His might, the plants a witness of His skill, the animals an example of His providence—the whole nature confirms He is wise and the entire world that its Creator is a devine and Almighty Lord. (p. 143)

Those members of the Indiana Civil Liberties Union who were evaluating the textbook and the background materials had no problem deciding that the use of the textbook in the public schools indeed appeared to violate the Establishment Clause of the First Amendment of the Constitution, and thus, the Fourteenth Amendment. It was further concluded that use of the textbook violated Article 1, Sec. 4, of the Constitution of Indiana, which states:

> No preference shall be given, by law, to any creed, religious society, or mode of worship; and no man shall be compelled to attend, erect, or support any place of worship, or to maintain any ministry, against his consent.

Additionally, it was discovered that the Indiana legislature had statutorily ordered that:

> The state board of education shall not approve a textbook which contains anything of a partisan or sectarian character. (I.C. 20–10.1–9–11, as added by Acts 1975, P.L. 240, Sec. 1, 1289)

Once having decided that the use of the biology textbook in the public school was beyond the pale both constitutionally and statutorily, there was still some controversy as to whether the ICLU should proceed with representing the complainants and taking legal action in the matter if necessary. The national office of the American Civil Liberties Union tried to dissuade its Indiana affiliate from proceeding. It was felt that such action could help undo some of the work of the ACLU in its many years of battling against censorship. Nobody would understand, the ACLU contended, any Civil Liberties Union fighting to ban the use of a book. Despite these protestations, it was nonetheless decided that the ICLU would proceed in the matter.

The initial step appeared to be to contact the Indiana Textbook Commission in order to voice and explain objections to the use of the biology book. Barbara Williamson, executive director of the ICLU, wrote to Dr. Harold H. Negley, state superintendent of public instruction, on July 29, 1976, indicating she was writing to him in his capacity as chairman of the Indiana State Commission on Textbook Adoption. She indicated that the ICLU had received requests for assistance from persons concerned about the use of the biology textbook and pointed out that the use of the same violated the First Amendment guarantees against the establishment of religion. She quoted from the Supreme Court decision in *Epperson* v. *Arkansas*, 393 U.S. 97 (1968) as follows:

> There can be no doubt that the First Amendment does not permit the State to require that teaching and learning must be tailored to the principles or prohibitions of any religious sect or dogma.

> The State may not adopt programs or practices in its public schools which "aid or oppose" any religion. This prohibition is absolute it forbids . . . the preference of a religious doctrine. . . .

She further indicated that attorneys for the ICLU would be happy to meet with members of the commission at their convenience. Dr. Negley replied to Ms. Williamson by letter dated September 7, 1976, indicating that the commissioners would be willing to meet with her or the ICLU representatives at their next meeting, which would be held on Friday, September 17, at 10:00 A.M. in Room 229 at the statehouse.

Appearing before the Textbook Commission at that meeting were Dr. John Bennet Olson, professor of biology at Purdue University, and Irving L. Fink. Objections to the book from both a scientific and legal standpoint were presented to the commission. When afterwards it appeared that no further action would be taken by the Textbook Commission for withdrawing the use of the biology book, the decision was made to file suit. The plaintiffs were Jon Hendren appearing by his next friend, Robert Hendren. Jon Hendren was at the time a ninth-grader in Silver Creek High School and had been assigned the biology book as a textbook. Other plaintiffs were Robert Hendren, individually, and E. Thomas Marsh. Mr. Marsh was a professor of fine arts at the University of Louisville and had children in Silver Creek High School and Silver Creek Junior High, and his younger child would have been assigned the textbook the following year. The defendants were Glenden Campbell, Betty Crowe, Harold H. Negley, Sterling M. Halton, Janet N. Wickersham, William Lyon, and Betty Lou Jerrel, who were sued individually and in their official capacity as members of the Indiana Textbook Commission.

While the official title of the case appears as *Hendren et al.* v. *Campbell et al.*, I have, for descriptive purposes, shown the case as *Hendren* v. *Indiana Textbook Commission*.

The other defendants were Ralph Guthrie, James L. O'Neal, Harold Nicholson, Robert P. Hauselman, and Charles E. Popp, who were sued individually and in their official capacity as members of the School Board of the West Clark Community School Corporation, which was the school system in which plaintiffs were involved.

The complaint bore the names of Lawrence M. Reuben, Richard D. Boyle, and Irving L. Fink as counsel for the plaintiffs, all of whom had volunteered their efforts in the case on behalf of the Indiana Civil Liberties Union.

The case was filed on February 8, 1977, in the Marion County Clerk's office and assigned as Cause No. S577–0139 to Superior Court Room 5, Honorable Michael T. Dugan, II, presiding.

The complaint requested an injunction enjoining the Textbook Commission from continuing to approve the use of the biology book, or mandating the commission to remove the book from its approved list as a textbook and enjoining the West Clark Community School Corporation from using the book as a textbook. Additionally, in order to obtain quicker relief, a request was filed for a preliminary injunction. The court ordered a hearing on the request for preliminary injunction on February 23, 1977, and indicated that the trial at that time would likewise consolidate the request for permanent injunction.

On February 11, 1977, William G. Mundy, deputy attorney general of Indiana, representing the members of the Indiana Textbook Commission, entered his appearance and also filed a Motion for Enlargement of Time to Plead to the Complaint. On February 16, 1977, James A. Lang, counsel for West Clark Community School Corporation members, filed an objection to the trial date and likewise requested a continuance. A Motion to Dismiss was also filed by both of the counsel for the defendants.

Among the grounds of the Motion to Dismiss was that the action was improperly venued in Marion County, inasmuch as the greater percentage of all the named defendants resided in Clark County, and that pursuant to Indiana Trial Rules the case should have been filed in Clark County.

The plaintiffs' counsel felt not only that there was legitimacy in the issue raised, but more importantly they did not want the case being tried in Clark County. A decision was made that appropriate relief could be obtained from proceeding only against the Textbook Commission, and a motion was filed on February 22, 1977, joining in the request to dismiss the action as it pertained to the members of the West Clark Community School Board. On that same date the court had ordered the Textbook Commission to submit written findings of fact concerning the alleged prior hearing, which had taken place on September 17, 1976.

In response to the court's order, defendants stated that there had been no administrative hearing on September 17, 1976, and therefore that there were no findings of fact which could be filed. In support of its response an affidavit of Harold H. Negley was filed which stated that the members of the commission who were present at that regularly scheduled commission meeting had indicated that it was not a formal hearing and that no minutes existed of that meeting.

In order to eliminate any issue, should the case be appealed, of whether there had first been an "administrative hearing" within the meaning of the law, it was agreed by all parties and the court that the court action would be continued pending a formal hearing before the Indiana Textbook Commission. That hearing took place on March 16, 1977, at the Terrace Room, ISTA Building, 150 West Market Street, in Indianapolis.

Meanwhile, the case was attracting wide attention. There were numerous letters to the editor in the press which continued for months after the case came to a conclusion. Calls were received from radio stations in England and Canada. A CBS television camera crew filmed taped interviews with various individuals involved in the case. That footage was later shown on CBS Morning News. Likewise, the case was discussed in *The United States Law Week*,* *Wall Street Journal*,** and *New York Times*.*** It was also discussed in an article in the *Yale Law Journal*.****

A minor conflict of sorts developed shortly prior to the hearing before the Textbook Commission between Dr. Negley and the plaintiffs' counsel. An accurate transcript of the hearing had to be submitted to the court. Dr. Negley insisted that the commission had no funds in its budget to provide a legal reporter, although he agreed that the tape recorders were not always reliable. As it turned out, the ICLU paid to have a legal reporter there for purposes of preparing a transcript of the proceedings, the accuracy of which could be sworn to. At the commencement of the hearing, in responding to a complaint that the commission was not providing a legal reporter, Dr. Negley stated that his department was running a deficit of $181,000.00, and he further stated: "If there is anyone from the Legislature here, I'd like them to hear that" (Tr. p. 4).

Counsel for the ICLU had decided that the most effective way of presenting the case before the commission was to have a collection of clergy of various denominations and faiths who would be willing to express criticism of the book as being a sectarian volume. Likewise, it was felt that counsel should present criticism of the book from a scientific standpoint from various university scholars in the field.

* 45 *Law Week* 2530
** *Wall Street Journal*, Jan. 17, 1978 (front page)
*** *New York Times*, April 24, 1977
**** "Freedom of Religion and Science Instruction," *Yale Law Journal* 515 et seq. (1978)

While there was a wealth of university science teachers willing and eager to testify, counsel had some difficulty in making clear to them that the ICLU was not taking the case merely because it was a poor biology book from a scientific point of view, and that without the religious objections to the book it would not be involved in the case. There was no constitutional right, it indicated, to the use of a good textbook. Counsel entered the hearing with an impressive collection of scholars, both lay and clergy.

The first witness called was Professor E. Thomas Marsh. He testified that he was a resident of Clark County, that he had children in the school system, that he was familiar with the biology textbook in question, and that he objected to the use of that book for his child. There was no cross-examination (Tr. pp. 6–7).

A second witness was William Mosley, a resident of Sellersburg, Indiana, and a biology teacher at Silver Creek High School. He testified that the Citizen-Teacher Committee of the school system did not recommend the adoption of *Biology: A Search for Order in Complexity*. He further testified that after the book was adopted by the school board, he along with other biology teachers attended a meeting to voice their protest at the adoption of the book.

He went on to state that all of the biology teachers in the West Clark County system were at the meeting and spoke against the book, indicating that they did not think that it was a suitable book for use in the school system. The school board then asked the protesting teachers such questions as "Are you a Christian?" and "Do you believe in God?" The book, he reported, was sectarian and not one of the better books (Tr. pp. 7–9).

On cross-examination, the witness said that in the teaching of biology he did not think the meat of the course was the subject of creation. Yet, he stated, that in his opinion the entire book was designed to push the one basic theory of biblical creation and steered more toward that than the meat of biology.

Witness Donald L. Nead, an ordained Presbyterian clergyman serving the University Church at Purdue, a *United Campus* ministry related to six different denominations, testified that the textbook did not represent his own Christian perspective. He further stated that in the seminaries of the mainline Protestant institutions—Presbyterian, Methodist, United Church of Christ, Christian Church, Disciples of Christ, certain elements of Lutheran, and the American

Baptist Convention—the understanding of the biblical record taught in the subject textbook had no longer been taught as a viable means of interpretation of biblical record for the past twenty-five to fifty years.

> It (the book) represents a very small segment of the Christian community that could uphold and support that. I think the vast majority of the Christian community would not agree with the position of that book. Therefore, I think it is a sectarian position (Tr. p. 18).

Another witness for the plaintiffs was Clark M. Williamson, professor of theology at Christian Theological Seminary in Indianapolis. Dr. Williamson presented a concise, scholarly, historical response as to why the biology textbook presented a religiously sectarian point of view (Tr. pp. 21–24).

Rabbi Jonathan A. Stein, then associate rabbi of the Indianapolis Hebrew Congregation, was asked about the use of a textbook in the public schools which openly stated that it seeks to maintain an educational philosophy or methodology consistent with traditional Christian perspectives. He replied that Jews have great allegiance to the ideas of separation of church and state. Jews have found that in those countries where the strictest possible separation is held, they flourished, and where church and state are merged, they often historically do not. He likewise confirmed that in his opinion the biology textbook presented a particularly sectarian point of view (Tr. pp. 20–30).

Dr. Robert G. Risk, a longtime president of the Indiana Civil Liberties Union, testified that he had for ten years formerly been on the national board of the Humanist Society. He further stated that the biology textbook presented a religiously sectarian point of view (Tr. p. 32).

The next group of witnesses called to testify for the plaintiffs were all scientists and educators.

Jon R. Hendrix, Ball State University biology teacher and a former high school biology teacher, helped write the guidelines for scientific instruction for the state of Indiana. He testified that the textbook was not within the guidelines. He further stated that as a person who professes a Roman Catholic tradition and as a biologist, he felt acceptance of a theory of evolution had nothing to do with a belief or disbelief in a God. He stated that it made no sense to base a textbook in science on a theory that "both God and the bible are beyond the proper method of study of scientists," as was stated on p. 427 of the textbook. Dr. Hendrix further stated that as a parent he would object to his children in public schools being taught from this textbook because it represents a very narrow theistic view (Tr. pp. 33–38).

Dr. John Bennet Olson, professor of biology at Purdue University, stated that he was authorized to speak for the Indiana College of Biology Teachers Association. On three occasions they had voted unanimously to request removal of the biology textbook from the list of approved texts in Indiana.

The book, he said, goes outside the scope of the subject of biology and into the area of doctrinary religious concepts.

> When you come to the sections on evolution . . . anyone who would be an evolutionist on the basis of concepts as presented there would be an idiot and I don't think that any bright high school student is going to be very much swayed by our biology if we say this is biology. I think this is idiotic. I think it does a bad job for biology and for science. . . .
>
> Creationism and evolutionism were in competition, of course, right after *The Origin of Species* was published, but creationism faded out and evolution grew. Why? Because it is right or wrong? No, because it is useful. It creates more science. Science comes to a halt when you think you have got the answer and when you don't have the answer you are constantly searching for it and science grows and evolution should not be judged as right or wrong. It should be judged as useful or not useful (Tr. pp. 38–42).

Sister Barbara Ann Burman, a member of the Order of Sisters of St. Francis at Oldenburg, was a biology teacher at Marian College. She testified that in her opinion one could be a good practicing Catholic and accept evolution just as well as an atheist.

> If I teach biology, I want to teach biology and not be bothered with teaching from the Bible. I believe that should go into the study of the Bible or in religious class. I can see some association but they are separate (Tr. pp. 43–45).

David Potter, a professor of neuro-science and zoology at Indiana University in Bloomington, testified that his opinion of the book, as a scientist, was that it was absurd.

I am most disturbed that the classroom situation exists where both students and teachers are faced with the book which I feel to be entirely inappropriate as a vehicle for the presentation of the science of biology (Tr. pp. 46–48).

Dr. Jane Kahle, associate professor of biology at Purdue and president of the Association of Hoosier Science Teachers, agreed that the book was objectionable from a biology teacher's standpoint and that it veered outside biology into religious sectarianism (Tr. p. 50).

Dr. Betty Allamong of Ball State University agreed that the book was bad biology and tried to place Christian beliefs and scientific theory on an even keel. The book, she indicated, is a Christian sectarian, fundamentalist book (Tr. p. 50).

The sole witness who testified in support of the biology book was Larry G. Butler, professor of biochemistry at Purdue and a member of the Creation Research Society. He testified that he had written one unit of the book and had gotten interested because he felt his own son's high school biology textbook gave an inadequate explanation of how we came to be, so he hoped to help in presenting a more balanced view. He felt that the textbook in question was adequate for ninth-grade biology classes. On cross-examination, when asked whether the book presented an educational philosophy and methodology consistent with traditional Christian perspectives, he responded that he did not know how to define traditional Christian perspectives but that it was roughly in accord with his own Christian perspective. (Tr. p. 56)

The Textbook Commission, despite the overwhelming testimony at the hearing, on March 18, 1977, in its findings of fact and conclusions of law, nonetheless determined that the textbook was not violative of the statute prohibiting the use of sectarian materials, nor of the constitutional prohibition of the constitutions of the United States and the state of Indiana. The request for withdrawal of approval of the textbook was thereupon denied.

The transcript of the hearing and the commission's findings were filed with the court, and the parties were given an opportunity to file briefs.

Counsel for the plaintiffs and for the defendants filed briefs with the court. Among the authorities cited on behalf of the plaintiffs were the following:

In *Epperson* v. *Arkansas*, 393 U.S. 97 (1968), the court said:

Government in our democracy, state and national, must be neutral in matters of religious theory, doctrine and practice . . . and it may not foster or promote one religion or religious theory against another or even against the militant opposite. The First Amendment mandates governmental neutrality between religion and religion and between religion and non-religion.

As the Supreme Court said in *Engle* v. *Vitale*, 370 U.S. 421, 432 (1962):

When the power, prestige and financial support of government is placed behind a particular religious belief, the indirect coercive pressure upon religious minorities to conform to the officially approved religion is plain.

The Court went on to quote James Madison, author of the First Amendment, who had written in *A Memorial and Remonstrance against Religious Assessments* (1784):

It is proper to take alarm at the first experiment on our liberties. . . . Who does not see that the same authority which can establish Christianity, in exclusion of all other Religions, may establish with the same ease any particular sect of Christians, or exclusion of all other sects? That the same authority which can force a citizen to contribute three pence only of his property for the support of any one establishment may force him to conform to any other establishment in all cases whatsoever.

In *Lemon* v. *Kurtzman*, 403 U.S. 602, 625 (1971), the Court stated:

The Constitution decrees that religion must be a private matter for the individual, the family and the institutions of private choice, and that while some entanglements are inevitable, lines must be drawn.

The brief filed by counsel for the Textbook Commission attacked the testimony of some of the witnesses of the plaintiffs on grounds they had testified that they had not read the biology book in its entirety. He further objected to any consideration of the book by the court on whether or not it was "good biology." He argued, despite the preface of the book itself, that the book clearly had a secular and not a religious purpose.

He, too, referred to *Epperson* v. *Arkansas, supra*, quoting from the concurring opinion of Justice Black as follows:

A second question that arises for me is whether this Court's decision forbidding a State to exclude the subject of evolution from its school infringes the religious freedom of those who consider evolution an anti-religious doctrine. If the theory is considered anti-religious, as the Court indicates, how can the State be bound by the Federal Constitution to permit its teachers to advocate such an "anti-religious" doctrine to school children? The very cases cited by the Court as supporting its conclusion hold that the State must be neutral, not favoring one religious or anti-religious view over another. The Darwinian theory is said to challenge the Bible's story of creation; so too have some of those who believe in the Bible, along with many others, challenged the Darwinian theory. Since there is no indication that the literal Biblical doctrine of the origin of man is included in the curriculum of Arkansas schools, does not the removal of the subject of evolution leave the State in a neutral position toward these supposedly competing religious and anti-religious doctrines? Unless this Court is prepared simply to write off as pure nonsense the views of those who consider evolution an anti-religious doctrine, then this issue presents problems under the Establishment Clause far more troublesome than are discussed.

Finally, Mr. Mundy, in his brief, quoted from the opinion of Justice Brennan in *Abington School District* v. *Schempp*, 374 U.S. 203, 300–301, as follows:

> To what extent, and at what points in the curriculum, religious materials should be cited are matters which the courts ought to entrust very largely to the experienced officials who superintend our Nation's public schools. They are experts in such matters, and we are not. We should heed Mr. Justice Jackson's caveat that any attempt by this Court to announce curricular standards would be "to decree a uniform, rigid and, if we are consistent, an unchanging standard for countless school boards representing and serving highly localized groups which not only differ from each other but which themselves from time to time change attitudes."

On April 14, 1977, Judge Dugan announced his decision. He had written a twenty-one-page Memorandum Opinion. Judge Dugan could have taken the easy path in this case. The overwhelming evidence against the textbook at the commission hearing gave him a sound basis for merely holding that the action of the commission, in concluding that the book was not sectarian, was arbitrary and capricious and should therefore be overruled.

Judge Dugan, however, chose to face the constitutional issues head-on. In his opinion he reviewed the testimony and exhibits presented to the commission. He quoted extensively from the text-book and the Teacher's Guide and concluded that while both the creationist and evolutionary viewpoints are mentioned, biblical cre-ation is consistently presented as the only correct "scientific" view-point to be considered. Two entire chapters, he pointed out, were devoted to disputing evolutionary theories and pointing out their fallacies and weaknesses. No chapters or passages in the text dealt critically with biblical creationism.

The court quoted extensively from various court decisions and discussed the history of developments in the area of church and state. Finally, the court bluntly stated that any doubts of the text's fairness were dispelled by the demand for "correct" Christian answers de-manded by the Teacher's Guide.

> The prospect of biology teachers and students alike, forced to answer and respond to continued demands for "correct" fundamentalist Christian doctrines, has no place in the public schools. The attempt to present Biblical Creationism as the only accepted scientific theory, while novel, does not rehabilitate the constitutional violation.
>
> After consideration of the text and the evidence at the agency hearing, the action of the Indiana State Textbook Commission is untenable. Government cannot be insensitive to the Constitution and statutes of the nation, and state. Their approval both advanced particular reli-gious preferences and entangled the state with religion.
>
> The decision of the Commission is without merit and violative of both statutory and constitutional provisions. (p. 20, Court's Memo-randum Opinion)

The court's official findings were as follows: (1) the findings of the Indiana Textbook Commission were arbitrary, capricious, and an abuse of discretion; (2) the findings were inconsistent with the evidence at the administrative hearing; (3) the findings of the com-mission were in violation with I.C. 1971 20–10.1–9–11, Article 1, Section 4, of the constitution of the state of Indiana, and the First Amendment of the Constitution of the United States; and (4) the textbook, *A Search for Order in Complexity*, as used in the public schools, violates I.C. 1971 20–10.1–9–11, Article 1, Section 4, of the constitution of the state of Indiana, and the First Amendment of the Constitution of the United States.

The findings of the Indiana State Textbook Commission were

thereupon reversed, and the commission was ordered to make findings not inconsistent with the court's decision after rehearing.

* * * *

It is not unreasonable for the question to be raised as to whether or why this case has sufficient significance to be dealt with in this series in observance of the bicentennial of the Constitution. The case, after all, involved only a decision of a lower court, inasmuch as the Indiana Textbook Commission did not see fit to appeal Judge Dugan's decision. I would submit that the significance of the case can be determined only against the background of those constant attempts made in our society to scuttle the effects of various court decisions preserving the constitutional separation of church and state.

The impact of the decision in the *Hendren* case was manifested in the very next session of the Indiana legislature. House Bill No. 1172 was introduced, which required that in any textbook where evolution was discussed there must likewise be balanced treatment for the teaching of special (biblical) creation. The bill, fortunately, did not pass, although the education committee reported it out with a "do pass recommendation." The Indiana bill was modeled after the Arkansas "equal time" statute, which was held unconstitutional in *McLean* v. *Arkansas Board of Education*, 529 F. Supp. 1255 (E. D. Ark., 1982). Similar statutes in Tennessee and Texas had likewise been adopted and were held unconstitutional. See *Daniel* v. *Waters*, 515 F. 2d 485 (6th Cir., 1975); *Steele* v. *Waters*, 527 S.W. 2d 72 (Tenn., 1975); and *Wright* v. *Houston Independent School District*, 366 F. Supp. 1208 (S. D. Tex., 1972).

Another attempt to inject religion into the public schools occurred from the introduction of a bill in the Indiana legislature requiring that every school classroom have a framed copy of the King James Version of the Ten Commandments. Nothing was said in the bill about discussing the Ten Commandments, only that the copy be hung on the wall. Apparently the sponsors felt that through some process of osmosis the morality of the Ten Commandments would seep into the characters of the students. The proposal did not get out of committee.

Currently, we are witnessing the present occupant of the White House bemoaning those decisions of the United States Supreme Court which outlawed prayer in the public schools. We have seen

Jerry Falwell and his supporters constantly berating the "godless" Supreme Court. On January 3, 1985, Senator Orrin Hatch of Utah introduced Senate Joint Resolution 2 for himself and Senator Dennis DeConcini of Arizona, proposing a constitutional amendment to permit voluntary individual or group silent prayer in the public schools.

The wall of separation between church and state of which Jefferson spoke appears constantly under attack. Nobody can safely predict what changes will occur in this area of the law with changes in personnel of the present Supreme Court. It can be safely predicted, however, that those forces in society which pushed for the use of the creationist biology book in the schools of Indiana, those who seek ways of overcoming the United States Supreme Court's decision prohibiting prayer in the schools, and those forces which see humanism as the cause for all our moral ills will continue their attacks against those constitutional safeguards of the First Amendment. I do believe that one effect of the textbook case is that no future Indiana Textbook Commission will ignore the constitutional prohibitions of the Establishment Clause.

I would like to share with you, with the permission of the author, parts of a letter written June 4, 1985, and sent to me by E. Thomas Marsh who, you will recall, was one of the plaintiffs in the textbook case. He is now distinguished teaching professor of fine arts at the University of Louisville.

> At the time of the textbook case there was, as you know, much media attention from many quarters. The Walter Cronkite team even came down to interview, and there was daily coverage in the local press and television. At that time we received several phone calls—always anonymous and usually late at night. Most were absurd like shouts of "Monkey, monkey, monkey!" and we were aware that we gained a reputation among fundamentalist groups as being tools of the devil. I suppose the worst thing was the pain caused my father who was a fundamentalist minister and felt so bitter that he totally disinherited me. As he has since died for the most part penniless, it has all worked out in its own ironical way.

> The greatest shock to me was the lack of support from local public school teachers. Perhaps there was fear of recrimination, but nonetheless it was puzzling.

Finally, there were amusing elements, i.e., we were marked, it seems, as fighters for causes in general so that for some time we received requests to help with all kinds of causes such as fighting against new band uniforms etc., etc.

From this hindsight vantage point I would do it again simply because it was a moral, civic duty. It was, however, not a pleasant thing at all. The recent political climate makes one fearful that such incidences are not likely to go away and also makes one appreciative of the Constitution and those like yourself who have been and continue to be willing to defend it.

*   *   *   *

If there were any heroes in the biology book case I would say we must point to Jon Hendren and his parents and Professor Marsh and his family who were willing to brave the insults and the pressures for standing up for a constitutional principle in which they strongly believed. I would also pay tribute to Judge Dugan who, as I pointed out, could have dodged completely any ruling on the constitutional issues and limited his decision to the arbitrary and capricious ruling of the Textbook Commission. For his thoughtful and thorough decision he deserves the gratitude of the public.

The American people will ultimately decide whether they wish to follow the views of an Edwin Meese or the poetic declaration of Justice Jackson in *West Virginia State Board of Education* v. *Barnette*, 319 U.S. 624, 642 (1943) when he wrote:

> If there is any fixed star in our constitutional constellation, it is that no official, high or petty, can prescribe what shall be orthodox in politics, nationalism, religion, or other matters of opinion or force citizens to confess by word or act their faith therein.

Never in our history, perhaps, has the First Amendment in the area of separation of church and state been under such fierce attack as we are now witnessing. Those of us who have strong feelings about the need to preserve these constitutional safeguards can draw courage from the actions of those who were willing to be plaintiffs in the *Hendren* case. Perhaps as never before we need to be reminded that particularly in this area eternal vigilance is the price of liberty.

Conceptualizing the Constitution: Lessons from and for Indiana History

David Ray Papke

Mr. Papke is Assistant Professor of Law and American Studies at Indiana University School of Law-Indianapolis. He is the author of Framing the Criminal: Crime, Cultural Work and the Loss of Critical Perspective, 1830-1900 *and "The Legal Profession and Its Ethical Responsibilities: A History," in* Ethics and the Legal Profession.

This essay is part of a collection, but it also differs in significant ways from the essays which precede it. Those essays are rich in facts, names, and figures regarding Indiana constitutional history, and each offers its own distinct lesson. This essay, by contrast, disdains extended historical narratives with conclusions and attempts instead to offer broad conceptualizations and examples. In this collection of essays, the essay at hand is a caboose at the end of a sparkling train, and as a caboose, the essay differs in form and function from what came before.

As for the essay itself, the central questions are straightforward but also quite broad. What is the United States Constitution? How might citizens of Indiana and of the United States best understand and conceptualize the Constitution? How might these conceptualizations guide and assist us in the future? In attempting to answer these questions, references to episodes and issues discussed in previous essays in this volume will be helpful. So, too, will be the development and use of three particular notions: the Constitution as icon, as text, and as law.

Icon

The first of the three notions—the United States Constitution as icon—is somewhat unusual and requires explanation. Icons may be easily pictured. They are most common perhaps in the Byzantine faith, but in that faith, as well as others, icons are carvings or paintings which symbolize the central figures and beliefs of a given faith.[1] They are physical objects and pictures which give expression to spiritual values and convictions. A carving of Christ on the cross is an icon with which many, but not all, Americans are familiar.

What does this notion have to do with the United States Constitution? In a special way the Constitution has over time taken on an iconic identity and come to symbolize central tenets of American faith. The "American faith," in this sense, is not Protestantism or Christianity. Indeed, it is not even a religion as it might traditionally be understood—an institution with houses of worship, clergy, and dogma. The faith is instead a general system of American beliefs which has been characterized by others as America's "civil religion." It is comparable perhaps to the *Romanitas* which somehow united or attempted to unite the disparate and differing populations of the Roman Empire.

Some have credited the French Enlightenment thinker Jean-Jaques Rousseau with first articulating the idea of a civil religion, but in American history it is the scholar Robert N. Bellah who has most consistently applied the idea to American experience. With support from a number of other scholars, Bellah has argued that in the decades following the Revolutionary War Americans developed a special optimism and confidence about the American way of life.[2] Undoubtedly, there were many who did not share this optimism and confidence—slaves, indentured servants, displaced Native Americans—but for white, male leaders at least, there developed a faith in the "American Way." There was a "civil religion," one which might not have been recognized as such in the era, but one which did function in ways similar to more purely religious faiths.

Certain developments of early nineteenth-century America add concreteness to the idea of a civil religion. It was during this period, for example, that some Revolutionary War leaders, participants in the Constitutional Convention and members of the first national governments, came to be thought of as "Founding Fathers." They were venerated because, in a paternalistic and semireligious way, they had established the nation. In a different time and setting, one might have expected to hear of a mother giving birth to the nation, but the patriarchal realities of the early republic precluded any such imagery. If the nation did not have a symbolic mother giving birth, it did at least acquire a birthday: the Fourth of July, which in this period became a national day of celebration. Americans also converted sites into veritable shrines: the Boston Common, Concord and Lexington, Yorktown, Mount Vernon, and Independence Hall in Philadelphia. Additionally, physical items became icons or emblems for the civil religion. There were the Stars and Stripes, the liberty pole, and the American eagle. The latter icon even caused controversy. Benjamin Franklin, himself one of the "Founding Fathers," had suggested that the plump and sturdy turkey be the American bird. Instead, Americans chose the sleeker and more majestic eagle, but to the dismay of countless turkeys ever since, the noble bird became a standard consumable guest at our traditional Thanksgiving feasts.[3]

In conjunction with these developments, the United States Constitution itself took on an iconic character. It became what that provocative but quirky scholar of modern life, Marshall McLuhan, has called "an audile-tactile form of resonant interface."[4] A less pretentiously erudite person might say the Constitution became an object which served as a mind mark in the American faith. It symbolized the values of the American civil religion.

One indication of the emergent iconic identity of the United States Constitution both then and, to a lesser extent, today is the manner in which individuals display and reproduce the Constitution. The original document itself is under the care of the National Archives, the custodian of federal records, and it is on display in hermetically sealed cases in Washington, D.C. Americans may stand before it and in the glow of special lights pray for the nation through the original.

For those unable to travel to Washington, D.C., and contemplate the original, there are also innumerable facsimiles and other reproductions of the United States Constitution. The facsimiles attempt actually to duplicate the original document. Many icons of the Byzantine faith were also reproduced as facsimiles, and scholars of these religious icons to this date have difficulty saying where and when they were made. Just as intriguing as the facsimiles of the Constitution are the more numerous special glorifying and memorializing pamphlets and books. These pamphlets and books do not appear as government documents or as appendices in textbooks but rather in forms which place the Constitution on a pedestal and which invite its veneration and, by extension, the veneration of the central tenets of the American civil religion.

The massive collection of the New York Public Library includes hundreds of these reproductions. They are somewhat concentrated in predictable periods: hundreds of such reproductions appeared, for example, at the time of the constitutional centennial in 1887 and again at the time of the sesquicentennial in 1937. Yet the reproductions are by no means limited to just these particular historical moments.

One quite striking flurry of iconic reproductions occurred in the early nineteenth century, in the so-called Early Republic and in the period when the civil religion became truly recognizable. In the years

1812–1830, many of these reproductions were the work of the ubiquitous Washington Benevolent Society. A patriotic organization with local chapters in dozens of cities and towns, the Washington Benevolent Society was an evangelistic wing of the civil religion. As the name of the society suggests, it was particularly proud of, and inclined to venerate, George Washington, the ultimate Founding Father and veritable godhead of the civil religion. Hence, the society frequently published short lionizing biographies of Washington as well as his Farewell Address, an address, incidentally, which was often known in the early nineteenth century as "The Paternal Address," a designation so much in keeping with the religious understanding of Washington as a father of the nation.

The Washington Benevolent Society and other groups and individuals also frequently reproduced the United States Constitution. These tidy, impressive little reproductions, like the carvings and paintings of saints and religious scenes in Byzantium, were icons for a dominant faith. Presumably, the constitutional icons were particularly important in Indiana and other parts of the country which were just entering the nation. The Constitution authorized Congress to admit new states, and, in keeping with the process spelled out in the Northwest Ordinance, Indiana could and did join the nation of states. More spiritually, citizens of Indiana could and did use the reproductions of the Constitution as inspiring icons.

Undoubtedly, the icons played a role in June of 1816 when forty-three men assembled in Corydon to discuss and draft a constitution for Indiana.[5] The convention was in session for eighteen weekdays, and it was hot within the blue limestone walls of the small county courthouse. As a result, the assembled frequently moved outdoors and met under the "Constitutional Elm" on Big Indian Creek. There was never any doubt that Indiana would be a free state rather than a slave state, but that question prompted arguments. So, too, did the less predictable question of who would receive the contract to reproduce and distribute the first Indiana Constitution. When the contract was awarded to Mann Butler, editor of the *Louisville Correspondent*, some were outraged. How could the contract be awarded to somebody from outside the state? The answer was less a matter of state pride than necessity. There was no other press close enough to Corydon.

As for the Indiana Constitution itself, a quarter of those present voted against even drafting it. Their fear, it seems, was that statehood would mean more taxes. The others were buoyantly enthusiastic. They drafted what in the time was one unusual provision: Article IX, which called for public schools and libraries and gave Indiana the distinction of being the first state to formally assume responsibility for educating its citizens. Beyond that, however, the convention copied significant parts of Articles I and III verbatim from the Ohio Constitution and other passages from the Kentucky and Pennsylvania constitutions. This was, among other things, practical, and many of the delegates hailed from these states. The Indiana framers also felt comfortable taking passages, sequences, and arrangements from the United States Constitution. The latter deserved to be replicated. It was a public icon.

Well after the Early Republic gave way to the Antebellum Period and to subsequent periods in American history, the replication and reproduction of the United States Constitution continued. There are in many periods reproductions which in their titles cast the Constitution as the "soul," "voice," "citadel," or "sentinel" of the nation—all spiritual images in a way.[6] Also, the Constitution has over the years on many occasions been published in special volumes along with different iconic partners.[7] So, for example, Thomas Jefferson's "Manual of Parliamentary Practice" often appeared alongside the Constitution, as did Andrew Jackson's "Proclamation of 1832" and Abraham Lincoln's "Gettysburg Address." For those anxious to expand the faith, to make it an Anglo-American affair, there have been numerous memorial pamphlets and volumes combining the Magna Carta and the United States Constitution.

Particularly intriguing as a form of combined reproduction are those numerous pamphlets and volumes including both the United States Constitution and the constitution of a given state. These publications suggest federalism, and they also suggest that the state constitutions resonate with the master icon.[8] Such publications have been frequent in Indiana, a fact which is in part explained by the laws of the Hoosier State.[9] The 1825 "Hierarchy of the Law Act" specifically places the United States and Indiana constitutions in tandem on a special plateau,[10] and the 1917 Indiana Constitutional Convention Act, Chapter 2, calls for the periodic joint publication of the two constitutions. More generally, the combined reproductions are indicators of the particular power of the constitutional icon and the civil religion as a whole in Indiana.

In the present historical juncture, the iconic use of the United States Constitution continues for Hoosiers and for citizens of other states. The nation has a Constitution Week and a Constitution Day, the latter being September 17. Neither is the most animated of national celebrations, but both spawn festivities and special events. The nation is also, of course, memorializing the Constitution in 1987, the bicentennial year. In these contexts and others, the Constitution remains today an emblematic expression of spiritual truth.

Consider three examples of the contemporary iconic power of the United States Constitution, examples from very different places on the political spectrum. One example, placed left of center, comes from the Indiana Civil Liberties Union, that determined defender of individual rights and freedoms. In a recent call for new members, the Indiana Civil Liberties Union in part actually reproduced the Constitution. It also called the Constitution "the most successful and enduring political instrument in human history" and declared that the organization's very purpose is the protection of this precious icon.[11] Closer to the political center is Sam Ervin, the garrulous senator from North Carolina who came to the fore during the Watergate investigations of 1973 and 1974. In his autobiography, published shortly before his death last year, Ervin wrote at length of his love of the Constitution and of his devotion to it.[12] Indeed, when choosing a phrase which would serve as the title of the autobiography and capture what he took to be the central motif of his life, Ervin settled upon "Preserving the Constitution." Placed to the right of Ervin on the spectrum, the Ku Klux Klan has also addressed the Constitution. In August of 1985 the Klan held a rally in Mansfield, Indiana. Perhaps many chose to look the other way, but a statement made at the rally by Jim Blair, the Imperial Wizard of the Knights of the Ku Klux Klan, was especially intriguing. Wearing his robe and pointy hat, the angry Blair told the assembled, "This Ku Klux Klan will support God; it will support the Constitution of the United States of America, and it will be for white people and white people only."[13]

It is troubling to hear the Imperial Wizard invoking the same icon as the Indiana Civil Liberties Union and Sam Ervin and doing so in a racist context. But there is also a lesson here. The United States Constitution as icon is symbolic. It does not, in this conceptualization, spell out the beliefs and attitudes which it symbolizes. Given the historical evolution of the civil religion and American political pluralism, the symbol may be invoked in different ways by different people in different times. Each individual in fact not only worships the beliefs behind the icon but also invests the Constitution with meaning. Since the civil religion is neither recorded as formal dogma nor in a more general way fixed and articulated, the constitutional icon is a vessel which can both supply and receive meaning.

Text

A second conceptualizing notion is the United States Constitution as text. This notion is more self-apparent than the notion of the Constitution as icon of the civil religion, but academics in particular will recognize what a potentially charged notion "the text" has become in recent years. An icon is the work of an artist or craftsman, and the contemplation of an icon involves worship. A text, by contrast, is the work of a writer or writers, and either in its original form or in subsequent publications, it must be *read*.[14]

Some consider the United States Constitution a difficult reading assignment, and as a result, certain authors and publishers have put together purportedly functional versions of it. These versions are supposed to make the Constitution easier to read, and they include Grace E. Brown's *Simplified Form of the Constitution*, Frank W. Phelps's *The United States Constitution Simplified*, and William S. McDowell's *The Constitution as It Is; A Logically Structured Compilation of the Constitution of the United States with Amendments Incorporated*.[15] There is, perhaps, some usefulness in these versions, but they are also mildly troubling. These efforts to make the Constitution more readable are something other than "the true text."

In fact, the United States Constitution is not really a difficult reading assignment. It is arranged into seven articles, and the four longest have conveniently numbered sections. The Constitution is something of an Enlightenment-inspired catalog or table, and its clear and systematic arrangement affords the reader easy access. Schoolchildren are routinely asked to read it in their classes, and teachers are so confident this can be done, they also ask children to memorize and recite what they have read.[16]

All of this sounds easy enough, but why, then, further explore the notion of the United States Constitution as text? The reason is that although most would agree the Constitution *can* be read, there is disagreement as to *how* it should be read. Does the text consist of precise words and sentences which can be read in and of themselves? Or is the text somehow more open to different readings by different people? This dispute has been central to many of the most important controversies in Indiana constitutional history. It is also, in a sense, the most pronounced ongoing controversy regarding the Constitution.

For evidence that this question is not trivial, it is unnecessary to look any further than several of the Indiana controversies discussed in previous essays in this volume. Our distinguished essayists do not necessarily discuss the controversies as ones involving how the United States Constitution was to be read, but a review of the essays illustrates that the question of how one reads the Constitution is central to each.

Take, for example, the *Ex parte Milligan* case, which was finally decided by the United States Supreme Court in 1866.[17] Attorney Alan Nolan's essay paints a sad and painful picture of Civil War Indiana in which state government came to a standstill and subversive traitors were perceived behind every tree. Against this backdrop and with the complicity of the Republican leaders of the state, Lambdin Milligan, a lawyer from Huntington and a leader of the state's Democratic Party, was tried, convicted, and sentenced to be hanged by a military commission. President Lincoln himself, who was in the midst of waging total war on the South, had authorized the commission and others to crack down on dissenters and those sympathetic to the Southern cause. Milligan sought a writ of habeas corpus, contending that the commission had no jurisdiction over him and that he had not been accorded a jury trial.

The United States Supreme Court ultimately agreed, but running throughout the litigation and appeals was a disagreement about how the United States Constitution should be read. Milligan and his attorneys were literalists. They pointed out that the text conferred the judicial power of the United States "in one supreme court and on such inferior courts as the Congress may from time to time ordain and establish," and they argued that military tribunals were therefore inappropriate for a civilian. Milligan and his attorneys also pointed to the exact language of the Fifth and Sixth amendments which guaranteed, respectively, grand jury indictment in capital cases and an impartial jury of the state. On the other side, meanwhile, were those inclined to read the Constitution and its amendments differently. Governor Morton and others urged a looser, less literal reading of the text. In wartime, they suggested, the Constitution became a different text. Parts of it could be suspended or even disregarded, given the severe threat to the nation by southern rebels and northern Copperheads.[18]

Another Indiana case which at least in part revolved around how the United States Constitution should be read was the more recent *Hendren* v. *Indiana Textbook Commission*.[19] Attorney Irving Fink, in his essay in this volume, presents the background and traces the litigation in that case. In 1975 the Indiana Textbook Commission authorized for use in high school biology classes a creationist book titled *Biology: A Search for Order in Complexity*.[20] Seven school districts then selected the book, but assorted parents and also the Indiana Civil Liberties Union protested in the courts. In the end, the latter parties prevailed because, in the opinion of Indianapolis Judge Michael Dugan, the Textbook Commission, in endorsing such a book, had violated the constitutional doctrine separating church and state.

Overall, this was a stirring victory for the parents, the Indiana Civil Liberties Union, and Attorney Fink himself, but in this case as well a dispute regarding how to read the text of the United States Constitution loomed large. Fink wanted the words of the Constitution read carefully and faithfully. In particular he pointed to the First and Fourteenth amendments. The former prohibits the Congress from making a law establishing a religion, and the latter applied this proscription to the state governments. The other side, meanwhile, was unwilling to read the so-called establishment clause as a total ban on *any* interaction between church and state. History, after all, includes many instances in which the nation has formally recognized religion: chaplains for the United States Congress, inscriptions on our currency, the Pledge of Allegiance, and so on. In the opinion of the Indiana Textbook Commission and the author of the controversial biology book, a rigid and literal reading of the Constitution was inappropriate. Ten years later the dispute echoes not only in subsequent textbook controversies but also in the raging debate regarding prayer in the public schools.

Some might be surprised to learn textual disputes were central in important constitutional cases in Indiana and in the nation as a whole, but the textual character of the United States Constitution makes such disputes inevitable. In a way, the Constitution resembles the Bible.[21] Among Christian churches and sects, there has long been a disagreement about how the Bible should be read. In some circles the Bible is a text which clearly conveys God's will through passages which may be read literally, through passages whose meanings and prescriptions are clear. Other Christian churches and sects, meanwhile, refuse to read the Bible this way. For them, its teachings must be supplemented and expanded.

In an analogous vein, similar disagreements haunt the reading of the United States Constitution. Is it a text whose words and meanings are to be strictly or loosely construed? Should readers approach it as determined textualists or willing supplementers? Are readers of the text to be interpretivists or noninterpretivists? With these basic questions as a seedbed, a whole second generation of perplexing questions has sprouted, and Americans have written hundreds, indeed thousands, of articles and books exploring reading problems relating to the Constitution.[22]

Textual questions of this sort will continue to develop in the future, but for purposes of this essay, a few simple observations are in order. On the one hand, some provisions in the United States Constitution are so literally clear they invite no reading problem. Article I, Section 3, for example, states that there are to be two senators from each state and that each senator shall have one vote in the Senate. Article II, Section 1 states that the president must be thirty-five years of age. But other clauses, sections, and amendments of the Constitution, on the other hand, invite loose construction. Provisions concerning trial rights, the separation of church and state, due process, equal protection, and the like invite debate, supplementation, and expansion.

Admittedly, this view results in a text which is more open-ended than some would like. Attorney General Edwin Meese would find this textual conceptualization of the United States Constitution nightmarish. For Meese, too many judges and individuals read the Constitution too broadly and are thus engaged in a form of "chameleon jurisprudence changing color and form in each era."[23] According to Meese, the framers chose their words and sentences carefully, and Americans must abide by their specific intent and textual language.

Justice William J. Brennan, Jr., by contrast, is a contemporary figure who has quarreled with Meese's statements on how to read the United States Constitution. Readers such as Meese, Brennan has asserted, are masking political biases of their own when they call for a commitment to literal language.[24] Brennan himself supports a more open-ended approach, and following his lead, readers may perceive the Constitution not as a fixed text out of which meanings are plucked but rather as a fluid text into which judges and average citizens may attempt to insert meanings. It is a text with which a reader may conduct a dialogue, and this interaction and shared searching may enrich both text and reader.

Law

A third and, for purposes of this essay, final conceptualization of the United States Constitution is a legal one. Law is in part icon and text. In respecting and worshiping the iconic law, Americans confirm their "lawfulness" and internalize the principles and beliefs on which the law is based. In reading the text of the law, they learn what divides the legal and illegal. But law is more than icon and text. It is, definitionally speaking, that which is "laid down, ordained or established" by the state, and as such, it has a pervasive public function. Law is the body of rules concerning action or conduct prescribed by the government, and more so than icon or text, law has powerful normative authority in social life. Lawbreakers are subject to formal sanctions and consequences.[25]

The United States of America may have some of the highest crime rates in the world, but Americans are also a people who have great confidence in the law. In particular Americans are proud of the United States Constitution as law and with justification look upon the Constitution as one of the greatest lawmaking accomplishments in history. Consider, in this regard, a statement from Justice David Davis in the Supreme Court opinion from the previously mentioned *Ex parte Milligan* case:

> The Constitution of the United States is a law for rulers and people, equally in war and in peace, and covers with the shield of its protection all classes of men, at all times, and under all circumstances. No doctrine, involving more pernicious consequences, was ever invented by the wit of men than that any of its provisions can be suspended during any of the great exigencies of government.[26]

Yet, conceding all of this, additional questions regarding the United States Constitution's legal identity emerge. The legal conceptualization, like the ones previously suggested, does not tidily solve all problems but rather points to new ones. Assuming the Constitution is law, what more can be said? What type of law is it? How does its exact legal character influence citizens' responses to it?

For German-speaking people, these questions might be somewhat easier to answer. The German language has a nice word for constitutional law, namely, *Verfassungsrecht*. Cut into halves and translated, the word is suggestive. *Verfassung* comes from the verb *Verfassen*, meaning to compose, tie together, or draft up. *Recht*, of course, means law. *Verfassungsrecht* thus means a composing law, a legal drafting up. It is the legal basis for a nation or a polity.

Perhaps the English word "constitution" conveys similar meanings. Constitutions "constitute," they bring things into being, but the notion of a constitutive law is vague and rarely contemplated by most Americans. More commonly, Americans think of the United States Constitution as "supreme law," but that too is vague and more iconic than instructive. The challenge remains: can Americans more specifically characterize the type of law which the Constitution is?

In American political history, there is one familiar legal understanding of the United States Constitution which appears. The framers of the document, for the most part, understood the Constitution as a "social contract." They were enamored with the social contract theory first articulated by the Greek Sophists and then further articulated during the Enlightenment in the writings of Hobbes, Locke, Rousseau, and Montesquieu.[27] Variations among these theorists are significant, but in general social contract theorists suggest that individuals in some sort of "state of nature" come together to form a "social contract." This contract becomes the basis of life together. It sets out the rules for social life, and individuals, for mutual convenience and survival, then live by the contract or compact instead of continually solving disputes on their own and "taking law into their own hands."

Americans might think of the social contract as both metaphorical and real. As metaphor, the social contract suggests a way that human beings come to live peacefully with one another. It suggests they are reasonable and able to cooperate. It is an appealing metaphor. On another level, the social contract for Americans is real, and it is the United States Constitution. After victory in the Revolutionary War, Americans were in a position to start anew. Our forefathers were in a position to draft an actual social contract for the new nation. An unsuccessful experiment with the Articles of Confederation followed, but the drafting and confirmation of the United States Constitution was a contractual undertaking. The Constitution was an actual contract or compact for American life.

Two hundred years later in time it remains useful to refer to this legal conceptualization. Social contract theory is hardly deceased; John Rawls, perhaps *the* most significant legal theorist of the post-World War II era, writes and thinks within the metaphor.[28] What's more, the United States Constitution, the nation's actual social contract, is of course still with us; it is, in fact, the oldest functioning written national social contract in the world. But still, Americans might remain alert for other types of legal characterizations which might be applied to the Constitution. Perhaps, in this regard too much has been said about the "death of contracts," a phrase made popular by the legal scholar Grant Gilmore.[29] He wrote of traditional contracts between specific individuals, the kinds formed by a meeting of the minds and based on legal consideration, and he argued that this classical contracts model was no longer operative before the courts. By analogy, the idea of a social contract may no longer be the best way to understand the Constitution's legal character.

An alternative legal conceptualization comes from University of Michigan law professor James Boyd White. Writing in his recent work *When Words Lose Their Meaning: Constitutions and Reconstitutions of Language, Character and Community*, White has suggested that we might understand the United States Constitution as a trust agreement, as a legal document similar to that employed in estate planning or in the establishment of a charitable institution.[30] The conceptualization is quite useful. It implies that the Constitution as law is not only a product of crisis and the founding of a new nation but also a plan which was supposed to guide those looking over the nation's interests in the years ahead.

Thinking of the United States Constitution as a trust agreement helps explain the doubleness of tone in the legal document.[31] The Constitution is, on the one hand, quite assertive and authoritative. Article I, Section 1, for example, says, "All legislative Powers herein granted *shall* be vested in a Congress of the United States, which *shall* consist of a Senate and a House of Representatives." The use of "shall" is imperative; the Constitution in this passage and others contemplates no variations. But just as frequently, the Constitution is merely suggestive. The Preamble suggests certain general purposes: the formation of a more perfect union, the establishment of justice, the insuring of domestic tranquility, the promotion of the general welfare, and the securing of the blessings of liberty. These are general goals for posterity, but the Constitution does not spell out in detail how they are to be achieved. In the case of Article I, Section 8, for example, the Constitution lists eighteen powers which the national legislature possesses, but it provides no concrete statements about how and when the powers are to be exercised.

All of this, White argues, is quite similar to the standard private trust. A trust document has some specifics, but it also tends to emphasize general goals and possibilities. The trustee, the person charged with seeing that the trust is lived up to, then does his or her best under the terms of the trust. He or she has a fiduciary duty. There are restrictions, but at the same time the trustee has freedom to exercise his or her best judgment. The trustee is assumed to be honorable, and the trust, in a sense, expresses trust in the trustee.

This is a pleasing way to conceptualize the United States Constitution. The document suggests a general way to look after the nation and its interests, but at the same time it gives the trustees power to make decisions and choices. Who are the trustees? Most commonly, they are the federal judges and especially the members of the United States Supreme Court. The framers may not have anticipated the large role which the judges would play as trustees, but they did in Article III create the federal courts. From the time of John Marshall in the early nineteenth century, the United States Supreme Court in particular has been prepared to understand itself as a trustee. Additionally, the legislature and the executive, the trustees created, respectively, by Articles I and II, have recognized and exercised their trusteeship. And then, too, there are the citizens. There is no article of the Constitution creating citizen trustees, but the Preamble is worded in a very interesting way. It begins, "We, the People of the United States. . . . " It does not say, "We, the United States. . . . " or "We, the elected officials of the United States. . . . " We, the people, have responsibilities to speak to the legislature, to advise the president, to take our controversies before the courts, and, most generally, to look after the interests of the nation under the Constitution as trust.[32]

John Marshall himself may not have thought of the United States Constitution as a trust in quite the way James Boyd White has, but White has underscored language from Marshall in the *McCulloch* v. *Maryland* decision which seems sympathetic to the trust idea. In trying to decide on the constitutionality of a national bank, Marshall said:

> A constitution, to contain an accurate detail of all the subdivisions of which its great powers will admit, and of all the means by which they may be carried into execution, would partake of a prolixity of a legal code, and could scarcely be embraced by a human mind. It would probably never be understood by the public. Its nature, therefore, requires, that only its great outlines should be marked, its importamt objects designated, and the minor ingredients which compose those objects be deduced from the nature of the objects themselves. . . . In considering this question, then, we must never forget, that it is a constitution we are expounding.[33]

All citizens, White argues, should be prepared to expound the Constitution, to say within certain boundaries what it does or does not make possible.

Conclusion

This essay has attempted to offer useful conceptualizations of the United States Constitution, conceptualizations which help us understand important constitutional episodes in Indiana history and which equip citizens for developments in the future. To be sure, there are conceptualizations other than the three which have been offered. But as for the three at hand, they are empowering. Understanding the Constitution as icon, text, and law does not estrange or alienate

individuals from the Constitution. Quite the contrary, these under-
standings provide pride and confidence in the Constitution.

In approaching the United States Constitution as icon, one need
not be an "iconoclast," that is, a smasher of icons. In the context of
our civil religion the United States Constitution is a tremendously
valuable symbolic totem of deeply felt belief. Icons in general, and
the Constitution in particular, are physical and visual items which
objectify the deep mythological structure of reality, help unlock the
mystery of our attitudes and assumptions, and bring order to chaos.
"When we can no longer draw from an icon bank," the scholar
Marshall Fishwick has argued, "we quickly go bankrupt."[34] We lose
magic and mystery in our lives. Our challenge, via the Constitution,
is to participate fully in American iconic life.

Secondly, in approaching the United States Constitution as text
one need be neither a text burner nor, to use a term which is popular
in contemporary academic circles, a "deconstructionist." The
United States Constitution is a text which we can and must read,
expand, and supplement. This reading experience, be it undertaken
in private, in the schools or universities, or in the courts, is dialectical.
By reading the text, we in a way read ourselves and our goals and
aspirations. We may through reading add meaning to the text.

Thirdly, in approaching the United States Constitution as law, we
need not feel unduly contained and straightjacketed. The Constitution's legal character is enduring yet amenable. We may think of it
as a social contract or a trust. Using the latter conceptualization, we
may appreciate the opportunity to influence the trustees of the
Constitution and be willing ourselves to serve as trustees. In participating in the legal trust, we may help shape the direction and
interests of the nation.

Overall, the United States Constitution as icon, text, and law is
wonderfully open-ended and fluid. If understood in other ways, as a
rigid, restricting document, it could be menacing. As a totally precise, preordained document, it could hinder speculative political
theorizing and social change. However, if we are willing to be wor-
shipers, readers, and trustees in the ways suggested by this essay, we
can through the Constitution participate in a creative, dynamic
national process. In Indiana and in the United States as a whole, we
can use the Constitution in the future to be believing, supple-

menting, caring actualizers of American life. The possibilities are exciting.

Notes

* My colleagues Gerald Bepko, Helen Garfield, and James Torke, and research assistant Anita Flax, kindly contributed to the shaping and refinement of this essay.

1. Standard studies of religious icons include Leonid Ouspensky and Vladimir Lossky, *The Meaning of Icons*, trans. G. E. H. Palmer and E. Kadloubovsky (1952; rpt. Boston: Boston Book and Art Shop, 1969) and David and Tamara Rice, *Icons and Their History* (Woodstock, N.Y.: The Overlook Press, 1974).

2. Robert N. Bellah, "Civil Religion in America," *Daedalus* 96 (1967): 1–19 and Robert Neelly Bellah, *The Broken Covenant: American Civil Religion in Time of Trial* (New York: Seabury Press, 1975); Russell E. Richey and Donald G. Jones, eds., *American Civil Religion* (New York: Harper & Row, 1974); and Catherine L. Albanese, *Sons of the Fathers: The Civil Religion of the American Revolution* (Philadelphia: Temple University Press, 1976).

3. David G. Orr, "The Icon in the Time Tunnel," in *Icons of America*, eds. Marshall Fishwick and Ray B. Browne (Bowling Green: Popular Press, 1978), 17.

4. Marshall McLuhan, "Further Thoughts on Icons," in *Icons of Popular Culture*, eds. Marshall Fishwick and Ray B. Browne (Bowling Green: Popular Press, 1970), 37.

5. For a discussion of Indiana's Constitutional Convention see William E. Nelson, *Indiana: A History* (1966, ppb. rpt., Bloomington: Indiana University Press, 1977), 91–96.

6. Representative titles include *The Voice of America: Our Constitution* (Los Angeles: G. W. Cartwright, 1925), *The Soul of America: Our Constitution* (Los Angeles: G. W. Cartwright, 1925), and *Sentinel of the Republic* (New York: Louis A. Coolidge, 1923). A secondary study suggesting an iconic characterization in its title is Randolph Leigh, *The Citadel of Freedom: A Brief Study of the Constitution and Its Builders* (New York: G. P. Putnam's Sons, 1923).

7. Representative titles abound. *The Political Memorial* (Concord, N.H.: G. Hough, 1827) contains the Constitution, Washington's "Farewell Address," and a biography of Washington. *National Jewels* (Philadelphia: A. Manship, 1865) contains the Constitution and speeches by Washington and Lincoln. *Great Words from Great Americans* (New York: G. P. Putnam's Sons, 1889) contains the Declaration of Independence, the Constitution, and speeches by Washington and Lincoln. *The American Trilogy* (New York: S. Graydon, 1939) contains the Declaration of Independence, the Constitution, and Washington's "Farewell Address."

8. The New York Public Library collection contains literally hundreds of these joint reproductions.

9. Joint reproductions of the Indiana and United States constitutions were issued by the Fort Wayne Printing Company in 1917 and 1936, by the William B. Burford Printing Company of Indianapolis in 1922 and 1934, and by C. E. Pauley and Company of Indianapolis in 1941.

10. Indiana Code, 1–1–2–1.

11. *The Advocate* (quarterly publication of the Indiana Civil Liberties Union), Fall, 1985:12.

12. Sam J. Ervin, Jr., *Preserving the Constitution* (Charlottesville: Michie Company, 1984).

13. *Indianapolis Star*, Spectrum Section, August 4, 1985.

14. A scholarly emphasis on "the text" was central in the work of so-called New Critics during the 1930s, 1940s, and 1950s. This school took its name from John Crowe Ransom's

The New Criticism (Norfolk, Conn.: New Directions, 1941), but it also counted among its practitioners the distinguished R. P. Blackmur, Cleanth Brooks, Allen Tate, Robert Penn Warren, and William K. Wimsatt. Formalists and the more contemporary structuralists are also, in their specialized ways, critics inclined to see the text as a self-sufficient object or as a world unto itself.

15. Akron: Grace E. Brown, 1932; Seattle: Brown & White Corporation, 1920; and Pittsburgh: Anderson and Grater, 1916.

16. The current Indiana Code requires that every public and nonpublic school provide instruction in grades six through twelve in the United States Constitution. Failure of any public school teacher or principal to comply with this requirement constitutes official misconduct. Indiana Code 20–10.1–4–1.

17. *Ex parte Milligan* 18 L.Ed. 281 (1866).

18. A similar "reading dispute" occurred during World War II when the federal government relied on military authorities to remove Japanese-Americans from the West Coast. *Korematsu* v. *United States*, 89 L. Ed. 194 (1944).

19. *Hendren et al.* v. *Campbell et al.*, Cause Number 577–0139, Marion County Superior Court, Room 5 (1976).

20. John N. Moore and Harold Schultz Slusher, eds., *Biology: A Search for Order in Complexity* (1970; revised Zondervan Publishing, 1974).

21. For further exploration of this analogy see Thomas C. Grey, "The Constitution as Scripture," 37 *Stanford Law Review* 1 (1984).

22. If we read the Constitution literally, do we read it as the framers would or as modernists might? If the former is correct, how do we know how the framers would have read it? If we read it as supplementers and expanders, what in a pluralist society are the bases and reference points? Can we refer to the overall structure of the Constitution, its most basic principles, or even to something totally external?

23. *New York Times*, November 15, 1985.

24. *Indianapolis Star*, October 13, 1985.

25. *Black's Law Dictionary*, Fifth Ed. (St. Paul: West Publishing Company, 1979), 795.

26. *Ex parte Milligan*, 18 L. Ed. 281, 295 (1866).

27. For an introduction to social contract theory see Ernest Barker, ed., *Social Contract: Essays by Locke, Hume and Rousseau* (New York: Oxford University Press, 1962).

28. John Rawls, *A Theory of Justice* (Cambridge: The Belknap Press of Harvard University Press, 1971).

29. Grant Gilmore, *The Death of Contract* (Columbus: Ohio State University Press, 1974).

30. James Boyd White, *When Words Lose Their Meaning: Constitutions and Reconstitutions of Language, Character and Community* (Chicago: University of Chicago Press, 1984), 244.

31. Ibid., 241–43.

32. Ibid., 240.

33. *McCulloch* v. *Maryland*, 4 L. Ed. 579, 601 (1819).

34. Marshall Fishwick, "Entrance," in Fishwick and Browne, *Icons of Popular Culture*, 5.

Index